ALL ABOUT ANGLING

ALL ABOUT ANGLING

by JOHN PIPER

PELHAM BOOKS

First published in Great Britain by
PELHAM BOOKS LTD
52 Bedford Square
London W.C.1
1970

© 1970 by JOHN PIPER

7207 0429 4

Printed in Great Britain by
Northumberland Press Ltd., Gateshead
and bound by Dorstel Press, Harlow

CONTENTS

CONTENTS

ILLUSTRATIONS

Photographs by Fish-Data Ltd.
Westbourne, Bournemouth

LINE DRAWINGS

FOREWORD

Angler's Mail was re-designed and launched by its new Editor, John Ingham, in May, 1966. Even by Fleet Street standards the transformation was amazing. Overnight, sales leapt from 19,000 copies weekly to figures in excess of 100,000, and they continued to rise. I wrote for that first issue as I have written, non-stop, for every issue since. Indeed, as this volume is published my contributions total almost half a million words—all about angling!

In 1966, as now, *Angler's Mail* provided a much-needed platform for those who realised that in such matters as the pollution of our rivers and coastal waters; the archaic organisation of fishery interests within the river authority system and of angling itself at that time, no improvement could be expected unless Britain's anglers were prepared to campaign and speak out in their own defence.

And campaign we did! On topics ranging from the commercial netting of immature sea fish to the lack of Government research when disease of plague proportions struck our salmon and coarse fish stocks. We gave the facts, commenting without fear or favour and spotlighting many a wrong that would otherwise have passed unnoticed.

When John Ingham first asked me to contribute to *Angler's Mail* he proposed that I should concentrate on developments in fish research, disease and allied subjects. I declined, and met with the inevitable query, 'What *do* you want to cover?'

'Give me carte blanche,' I said, 'to write about anything and everything likely to interest our readers.

I often relive the silence that followed and count it one of the highlights of my career—and my own good fortune—that John decided as he did.

Of course I have written about my own fishing, many times, as every other angling journalist has done. But I have also been able to report on other people's ideas and their approach to this sport of ours; on tackle developments and fishery management techniques, new trends and knowledge from centres as far afield as America, Japan and the Iron Curtain countries. Although writing provides my livelihood—a tougher job than many people imagine—gathering this material has proved a fascinating occupation.

Most experienced anglers will agree that there is more to the sport than the catching of fish. If this selection of articles from my first four years with *Angler's Mail* (1966-1969) conveys something of the range of interest, excitement and relaxation to be achieved with a rod, it will have been worth while.

I find it impossible to worry beside a river or lake, or while fishing from a boat or the sea shore. In this I am not alone. It may be that as the pressures of modern living increase so more people will discover that going fishing is cheaper and in every other way preferable to consulting one's doctor or psychiatrist, and far more sensible than developing ulcers. The Government and angling's own representatives must ensure that clean water and quality fishing abound for all to enjoy. For who can doubt that with sound management, revision of the laws governing our outdated Close Season, and the inclusion of certain inshore waters within the National Parks network, there need be no shortage of such facilities. We in Britain should be the proud possessors of the finest sportfishing in the world.

I cannot close this Foreword without thanking the many friends who, in their various ways, have made this book possible. If they are too numerous to mention by name that, too, is my good fortune. But like most law-abiding anglers I have only one wife. For the packed lunches, the patient repairing of torn jackets and overtrousers, and for tolerating a man to whom any hour of the day or night can signal good fishing weather, this brief acknowledgement is quite inadequate, but none the less sincere.

JOHN PIPER

PART ONE
OVERSEAS

TWENTY MILES OF ICE

Within two minutes' walk of Charing Cross a small wine house does a thriving trade for which it has no licence—an unusual state of affairs tracing back to the year 1364 when Edward III granted Royal Letters Patent to the Free Vintners. I was there one lunchtime, enjoying a glass of wine, when a complete stranger put a question out of the blue, a question voiced in a pleasant but unmistakable Canadian accent.

'Excuse me, but are you a fisherman?'

I wondered for a moment if I'd grown fins or left a No. 8 hooked in my lapel. In fact, George Rickard, 47-year-old Toronto resident over here for a short holiday, had spotted my ACA tie. For the next two hours we talked fishing. In particular, we talked of ice fishing on Canada's Lake Simco in temperatures that make an English winter seem more like high summer in the Med. The mercury moves from 30 above to 30 below zero, with 18 above as an average reading. In such conditions, maintained on Lake Simco for three months of every year, ice fishing becomes a practical proposition.

There's no question of venturing a few yards from the bank and knocking a hole in the surface. The lake is 20 miles wide and the ice sets solid to a depth of 27 in. right the way across. Ex-Army Snow Weasels carry parties of anglers over this wide, white highway, their rubber-tracked wheels powered by engines generating 200-300 h.p. and travelling at a cruising speed of about 30 m.p.h. Let's climb aboard.

Four or five miles out the Weasels reach a group of tiny huts, each equipped with a seat, a stove-pipe chimney and a hole in the ice. And as the party gets ready to fish, a mere 27 in. of frozen water separates men, huts and vehicles from depths plunging to 100 ft. and more.

By now it's 7.30 a.m. With a biting wind blowing non-stop you make for your allotted shack as quickly as possible. I'm told that Ukranians who have settled in Canada rate these huts an unnecessary luxury, preferring to fish in fur coats and fur hats, oblivious to wind and weather as they balance on miniature fishing stools. Less hardy types need some protection. Inside the hut, pitch darkness slowly gives way to the pale light reflected through the ice; you put a match to the stove, fill the teapot, and before long it's warm enough to remove coat and gloves. And then you start fishing: the quarry, whitefish. These are bottom feeders scaling $1\frac{1}{2}$-2 lb. The occasional lake trout comes in as a bonus, with a pike of 25-30 lb. guaranteed to create chaos in such a confined space.

Rods play no part in this type of angling. Eight-pound nylon is wound on a stick slightly longer than the width of the ice holes. Baited with live minnows on a two-hook paternoster, the line is paid out until the lead touches bottom and the stick or 'teeter' can be rested across the hole. Your eyes play tricks as you decide whether to strike or not, for whitefish are dainty feeders and those tiny livebaits can also make the stick teeter and tremble. The chances are that when you do strike you'll be into a fish that will fight every inch of the long haul to the surface.

Through the summer months George Rickard and his pals fish for the largest of the world's pike, the muskellunge. For this beauty there's a size limit of 28 in. in Toronto waters. Black bass, our own northern pike and walleye or zander add to pre-winter sport. Canada's lakes and ponds are constantly being surveyed, sampled and restocked, and the fishery laws are not easily broken. Close seasons really are closed seasons; anyone caught with a fish in his car—out of season—loses the fish, tackle and the motor car!

Just before we parted, George told me how his family had emigrated from Watford when he was a mere seven-year-old. 'I've enjoyed my fishing,' he said, 'but we had more luck as kids than I've ever known since buying a lot of fancy equipment.'

It's a sentiment many will share with him. Did you ever tickle small trout; catch miller's thumbs in mud harbours hand-built in the shallows; land your first mighty roach—all of 3 oz. as I recall—on a 'rod' that should have been propping up the Old Man's chrysanthemums? And did you ever manage to get all the mud off your pants before daring to return home? As a small boy in Watford, and later still in Canada, George Rickard never found the answer to that one. For that matter neither did I.

CATS ON A HAYHOOK

How many catfish are there? I doubt if many people know the precise figure, but of one thing we can be sure—there are well over a thousand species of this shovel-headed brute ranging across the globe. They include a South American 'cat' so small that it lives in the gills of other fish. They include giants from the Danube basin, weighing several hundred pounds each. But the sea catfish or wolf, taken around our coasts, bears only a superficial resemblance. It is not a true catfish.

The monster European cats, up to 10 ft. in length, are said to be the most long-lived of all freshwater fish, with an estimated age limit of 60-70 years. As Bill Keal once said, 'You either love 'em or hate 'em!' I've never fished for cats and I don't particularly want to, but they are now firmly established as part of the angling scene and many anglers, especially in America, concentrate on this one species. Over there the reason is not hard to find. The so-called channel catfish, one of 36 kinds in Canada and the USA, is a gourmet's delight. If an American angler has to choose between returning a trout or a channel cat to the water the chances are that the trout will survive. Catfish stew is one of the world's great delicacies.

Best known of all catfish venues in the United Kingdom is Woburn Park, Bedfordshire. Wels—Danubian catfish—have flourished there since 1880, but reached this country for the first time nearly 20 years earlier. In 1862 or 1863, 36 specimens were imported, 10 being released at Aldermaston Park, Reading. The odd thing is that none of those caught since that time have matched the tremendous weights common to their native waters. What, I wonder, accounts for this difference in growth rates?

The ancient Egyptians knew all about freshwater catfish. As far back as 3,000 BC they recorded the presence of raab, the thunder fish. It is well-named, for that particular species generates a fierce electric shock. But the Americans have more experience of cats than any anglers yet raised in these islands, although the species is said to be spreading over here and within a century it may be relatively common. A menace? I doubt it. You may think such a fearsome-looking brute could hold its own with anything that swims, but the male catfish is said to be something of a cissy. True, he guards the nest until the eggs hatch, but a determined raider will often drive him sufficiently far away to be sure of snatching a quick meal. And when the young are born they hang in a tight-packed school, easy prey for any predators in their stretch of water.

Jack Kemmerer of *Field and Stream* swears that 'some catfish fanatics won't use anything but a hay hook—a heavy, short hook found on most farms and used for handling bales of hay'. These hooks are baited with red flannel, tied to a 40 ft. hand-line and played beneath overhanging banks and other spots favoured by the blue catfish. Using such tackle, one man hooked the same fish three seasons running. Not only did he fail to land it, but the fish was so big that on each occasion it nearly drowned him. Finally, with something of a love-hate relation-ship bubbling between them, the angler succeeded. He hay-hooked, handlined and landed a cat weighing 110 lb.

Stinkbaits hold pride of place with American anglers, the term covering an incredible range of garbage. For the benefit of visitors to Woburn and other British venues I report that baits on the Highly Commended list include aged rabbit livers, congealed blood, rotted beef spleens and yellow laundry soap. Rotten minnows, mould cut from over-ripe cheeses, soured clams and high salami are proven cat-getters.

And since the Yanks have such a marked advantage among

catfish hunters, I'll stay with them for my finale on this particular subject. A method known as 'grabbing' is practised in several States—a nightmare variation on tickling trout. The drill is to find a male catfish guarding its nest, reach slowly into the water, grab the fish, thrust one arm through its gill cover and out through the mouth, then 'Heave-ho!' It sounds too fantastic for words, but the method is illegal in many parts and it takes fact not fantasy to formulate State laws. As a matter of authentic record, catfish up to 40 lb. have been landed in this way.

FISH THAT DREAMS ARE MADE OF

Supertrout are migratory—anything but ideal for lake or reservoir. Reports that this fabulous new gamefish results from crossing rainbow trout and chinook salmon are quite inaccurate, although research involving the new fish and the chinook is under way. I'm told that the end-product may have profound implications for the food supply of the human race. But the supertrout itself springs from a breeding programme between fast-maturing stay-at-home rainbows and their close relatives, the migratory American steelhead trout. These two, plus the high standards of selection insisted on by Dr. Loren Donaldson, professor of the College of Fisheries, University of Washington, have produced a gamefish of record-shattering proportions.

This magnificent trout is stronger, less prone to disease and pollution, and capable of producing 10 times more eggs than the average brook trout—one returning three-year-old shed more than 20,000 eggs.

Year-olds have been weighed at 3 lb.; two-year-olds at 7-11 lb., and fish in their third year an incredible 17.5 lb. What weights will they reach eventually? 'I don't know,' said Dr. Donaldson in 1969, 'they haven't stopped growing yet.' (See Plate 16.)

Fingerlings are fed for six months on a special diet of predigested hake, then released into the University's lake at Seattle to make their way down the ship canal. Twelve thousand were turned out in 1965. They journeyed seawards, returning to spawn after one year in the salt, weighing 1½-2½ lb. more than normal steelhead sea trout of the same age. From that and other releases a major breeding stock has been established and as they come back the fisheries staff face the unenviable task of sorting and grading half a million supertrout to select 200 prime specimens for future programmes.

Some indication of the strength of that migratory urge may be judged from known facts concerning the parent steelhead stock. These have been tagged far out at sea and later recovered as they approached spawning beds 2,500 miles away. Steelheads spend their ocean life feeding on squid, fish and even small birds plucked from the surface.

But to return to the supertrout—and that, by the way, is its official name—a great deal has yet to be done before stocks are available for sportfishing purposes overseas. If they ever do reach us; if they are able to survive in our waters, where will it be? The chalk streams of Hampshire? ... The rivers of the West Country? ... The West Coast of Scotland? You choose!

THE FISH THAT COULD NOT EXIST

Early in 1968 the world lost a dedicated scientist and an angler of no mean skill. He was also the greatest specimen hunter of all time. On January 8, teleprinters linking the South African port of East London with agencies all over the world chattered out the news that, at 70 years of age, Professor J. L. B. Smith was dead. Tragically, this man who devoted his life to the study of fishes—nearly half of it to one species—died by his own hand.

His fish was the coelacanth, thought to have become extinct 50-million years ago. (If the name looks a tongue-twister pronounce it 'seel-a-kanth'.) The Professor was responsible for finding and identifying the first two specimens. Something like it just had to happen. From an early age he dreamed of discovering a primeval swamp untouched by progress and inhabited by creatures of pre-historic days. In the link between the quiet, independent scientist and the coelacanth—a species that has survived 300-million years—there seems more than a hint of pre-destiny. For the full story you must read his book, *Old Four Legs*; I can give no more than a sketch of that incredible adventure.

A qualified chemist, seriously ill for much of his life, Professor Smith burned up enough energy for 10 men. He devised a numerical system of fish identification, published scientific papers, wrote for the angling Press, fished with his dog Marlin always in the prow of his boat, and badgered the trawler skippers to keep unusual catches for his inspection. But the trawler crews were not interested. 'So,' wrote Smith, 'I endured the miseries of small trawlers on South Africa's stormy seas, often so seasick as barely able to crawl along the slippery, heaving decks to scratch among the slimy rubbish shoved aside. To the crews I was no longer a remote scientist who expected them to do his dirty work. They changed from indifference to interest; sometimes enthusiasm.'

The stage was set. On December 22, 1938, Miss Courtenay-Latimer, the young and energetic curator of the East London Museum, received a 'phone call to say that on just such a trawler a pile of fish awaited examination. They were mostly sharks, but one was different, of an odd shape. It was 4½ ft. long, 127 lb., heavily scaled and blue in colour. Its fins looked like limbs gone wrong.

Miss Latimer had no means of identifying it, but she had the fish set up and sent sketches and notes to Professor Smith. He wrote later of his reaction to that letter. 'I turned the page and saw the sketch, at which I stared and stared. It looked more like a lizard. And then a bomb seemed to burst in my brain and I was looking at fishes no longer here, fishes that had lived in dim past ages. I told myself sternly not to be a fool, but ...'

Long after his positive identification other 'experts' were unconvinced. 'He must be crazy,' said one. 'At best the specimen could only be a rock cod with a mutilated and degenerate tail.' Unhappily, the soft organs had been disposed of before Smith could reach the Museum, and those organs—brain, stomach, heart and liver—were vital to his work at that moment. From then on, the search for another coelacanth became an obsession. The 14-year saga is one of suspense and frustration, of real-life adventure and a driving determination that few people could match or maintain. Year in, year out, he battled with the authorities for funds, for help of any kind that would enable him to pinpoint the home of the coelacanths and obtain an entire specimen. This was imperative. Fossil remains rarely give much indication of the soft anatomy of the creature concerned and the discovery of a 'living fossil' such as this was in every sense of the word, sensational.

Dr. Smith and his wife travelled thousands of miles. They distributed leaflets offering rewards; they fished and talked with men of the sea, always seeking the coelacanth. At the same time they collected more than 10,000 marine specimens, many of them rare, for various museums. It was tough work and as it drew to a close in December, 1952, Eric Hunt, skipper of a schooner trading in the French Comores, telegraphed news of coelacanth No. 2.

This specimen differed from the first. Hooked on a long line at 20 fathoms, it had no front dorsal fin. The French, realising its value, threatened to impound it. Time was desperately short if the brain and other organs were to be saved, and just to make matters worse, Smith had no way of getting to his precious coelacanth—if that is what it was. It can be hell-hot in the Comores: fish go off quickly, even those partially injected with formalin. The Professor tried every Government official who might enable him to fly out and collect the 90 lb. fish. None would. At last, fearing a point-blank refusal, he 'phoned the Prime Minister, asked for a Dakota of the RSAAF, and got it.

One can only imagine his feelings during the flight out and those as the plane took off, with the coelacanth aboard, on the return trip to South Africa. Smith's case was proved; the coelacanth's niche in the record of evolution was established beyond doubt and the fantastic search for a living fossil, for a fish that could not exist, was over. Two fish in 14 years—specimen hunting of the highest order!

SALTWATER PLUS:
FRESHWATER MINUS

When American angler Charles Cinto sailed into Vineyard Sound on June 16, 1967, he little guessed that this blustery evening was to be the greatest any bass specialist could hope for. A strong sou' westerly was blowing and a heavy sea running as the 25-foot charter boat carried Cinto and a friend towards their first fish.

The striped bass of American waters is larger than our own, but closely related. As in this country, it attracts a band of dedicated enthusiasts—the big-bass hunters. Charlie Cinto paid out 50 ft. of line carrying a 10 in. plug, blue-backed, white-nosed, its belly flecked with red. Then he struck the fish bass anglers dream about. After a battle that warrants a chapter to itself, Cinto boated a specimen 'striper' weighing exactly 73 lb., matching to the ounce a world record that had stood unchallenged for more than half a century.

Oddly enough, two days before I read the American report I'd been chatting with John Goddard of Efgeeco. As the Company's Managing Director, John roams the world in search of new tackle, new and practical ideas. And wherever he goes his rods see action. He, too, had noted the way bass specialists use plugs in the United States.

'They do a lot of surfcasting with plugs,' he told me. 'Particularly surface plugs. It's exciting sport. When the fish take they invariably come right out of the water. It might be worth trying over here.'

Those plugs have scooped noses, designed to 'pop' through the surface water. They range from 6-10 ins. long, weigh anything from 4-8 oz. and feature in casts averaging 80-90 yds. I put the obvious question. 'How would you compare British and American angling?' He grinned. 'I'll answer that if you promise to stress the fact that I'm generalising. Freshwater fishing out there is generally coarser; sea fishing generally very much lighter than our own.'

Their different approach to sea angling is due to two factors. Americans are far more record conscious than we are, and their record list is so arranged as to encourage a wider range of techniques. The International Game Fish Association bases its records not only on species, but on the strength of line used to capture a particular fish. For each species there are records relating to breaking strains from ultra-light to extreme heavy-weights.

Did John Goddard think we could benefit by adopting the same procedure? 'I'm sure of it,' he said. 'The majority of our sea anglers fish far too heavy; sport might be very much improved. It would promote more interest, a greater variety of techniques and a lot more skill.'

Just back from a five-week trip to Canada and America, John had fished for striped bass, marlin, walleye (zander), catfish, large- and smallmouth black bass, and the little yellow perch of North American waters. The marlin session has pride of place in his diary, for of all the fish in the whole wide world this one is the most difficult to hook. Unlike others of its family, the white marlin rarely strikes the bait with its bill, warning the angler of its presence. It approaches from behind, takes the bait in its mouth, feels the line and lets go! You have to spot the fish, anticipate the moment when it opens its mouth, give slack line and then hit it. Release line too soon, strike too soon, and you'll be minus another white marlin.

The prestige of the marlin boats depends on their clients' records. A crew member normally strikes the fish, gets it well on and only then hands the rod to the passenger to play and claim any specimens taken. Not for John Goddard. After a few determined words with the skipper it was agreed that this angler would handle his own rod throughout the proceedings. That same day he boated a 55-pounder.

Freshwater ... 'The most astonishing things,' said John, 'are the floats they use. They're like bungs, even those intended for tiny fish. Small floats seem to be unknown.'

He told me of the interest shown in his 'miniature floats'. Miniatures? For the most part he was using medium-sized Avons.

As to the fishing, he found smallmouth bass vastly superior to our own perch, their fighting qualities on a par with rainbow trout. They tend to do battle at the surface and they jump like mad. What a fish it would be at selected venues over here, if —and that 'if' is almost insurmountable—if only our climate and water temperatures were more suitable for them.

Canada offers wonderful fishing. Vast lakes, thick with trout and pike, with bluegill and others in such numbers that the main problem is getting the bait down to the big fellows. In this respect, John Goddard found some waters quite frustrating, but I noticed that his bag for the trip included a 13 lb. catfish, played out on 4½ lb. line and a light glass rod—not bad fishing! Final word from this roving angler: 'Their freshwater angling is often crude by our standards. Any experienced British angler could quickly become a leading authority, our techniques are so far ahead. But as I said before, I'm generalising. Believe me, there are exceptions!'

ZANDER FACTS FROM FRANCE

The August, 1967, issue of the French angling monthly, *La Peche et Les Poissoins*, was a holiday special. But in France the zander controversy was already under way. The Editor felt bound to interrupt his bright-sun-and-blue-water theme with a special reference to this predator.

'This fish,' he wrote, 'is fairly new to our waters and has been

widely discussed recently. A voracious eater of small fish, especially of bottom fish such as gudgeon, the zander de-populates
the rivers in which it breeds. The National Council can envisage
the need for restocking with small fish in the zander areas, but
has decided to limit such restocking to previously polluted
waters.' The point being, of course, that at these venues the
zander will almost certainly have been wiped out. The smaller
species will thus have some chance to re-establish themselves.

It seemed clear from the remainder of that editorial that the
zander had divided the French angling fraternity into two
camps. In another issue of the same year, M. Gaston Perche presented a most detailed and interesting comparison between
known facts concerning the zander—introduced to France from
Central European countries—and the pike. The zander prefers
calm waters; wide, deep and relatively warm. A much lower
growth rate is evident in cold, fast-flowing rivers. He quoted
3-5 metres as the ideal depth, with a maximum of 10 metres.
Gravel and sandy bottoms are preferred and the fish reaches full
development in lakes with this type of bed.

Its vision is adapted to life near the bottom and to survival
in coloured waters rather than gin-clear streams. Indeed, the
point is made that 'to our knowledge it has never been seen, as
has the pike, in trout waters'. This, at least, is heartening news,
though not for such fisheries as Grafham and Weir Wood. And
before the game fishermen of England throw their hats in the
air let me add that zander are well-established in the grayling
stretches of the River Rhine—in a sector of that river featuring
pure water, generally deep, with a hard bottom of sand and
gravel. M. Perche also noted that where zander colonise alkaline waters the other species are quickly wiped out.

This fish shoals strongly in the mouths of rivers and, like the
perch, appears to be attracted to wharves and similar man-made
installations. It can survive well in dirty water and in estuary
stretches with a maximum salt content of 9 g. to the litre, but
is very susceptible to pollution. By comparison, pike are said to
tolerate no more than 3 g. of salt per litre of water.

At birth, the zander alevin is extremely small, transparent

and almost invisible; growth in the early stages is slow and in lakes and ponds unprotected eggs are greatly reduced by feeding roach—a form of predation observed on many occasions. The average number of zander eggs is given as seven times more than those of the pike and the proportion of the sexes is quoted as 15 per cent male, 85 per cent female. With fish of the same length, M. Perche found the zander heavier than pike, although the pike's average growth rate is faster. Not surprisingly, male zander have a lower growth rate than the females. He also confirms the species' low resistance to shock, handling and transportation hazards.

Zander shoal until 4-5 years of age, at which stage the tendency to move in smaller groups is noticeable. Like our own perch—a smaller member of the same family—the really big fish are 'loners' and these tend to hug the river bed. In this context the term 'really big' is no exaggeration; under the heading of exceptional specimens zander of 33-44 lb. are listed—more than 5 lb. heavier than the largest pike in the records used.

Zander Reproduction

Month	April
Water temp.	+12° C.
Sexual maturity	3 years (35 cm. 380 g.)
	4 years (43 cm. 750 g.)
Mating unit	1 male, 1 female
No. of eggs per kg. of female's weight	200,000
Diameter of eggs	1.5 mm.
Colour of eggs	Grey and sticky
Spawning sites	Brickwork, branches & water weed
Incubation temp.	+12° C.
Alevin at birth	3 mm., transparent

How long do they live? M. Peche suggests a life span of 14-15 years and quotes Prof. Pannetier's findings indicating that in the River Saone, rated the best in France for roach and other cyprinids, the zander's growth rate was 3-4 times greater than the average in other parts of the country.

These are the facts so far. No one need doubt that zander will in time equal the average weight of Britain's pike, or that specimens at the higher end of the growth scale will do likewise. Meantime, I'm going grayling fishing!

UPTURNED TAILS

FIG. 1   *Keel hook*

That odd-looking shape is the fly hook of the future; a shape making many of the Trade's vast stock of straight-shanked, down-turned hooks positively obsolete. I'd like to tell you that these self-protecting, weed and bushproof fly hooks are 100 per cent British—a new design by Tom Jones of Northampton, made by Bulldog Tackle of Birmingham and approved only after a season's trials on Test, Tey and Tor. That's what I'd like to tell you. In fact, the keel hook is an American idea, and a brilliant one.

Experts who have tested this unique design sing its praises in no uncertain manner. Al McClane, one of few anglers with a truly international reputation, considers it one of the most significant developments in fly-fishing for many years. He writes: 'Ever since the legendary Dame Juliana Berners placed her square-headed needle in a red-hot charcoal fire, hook bends have pointed south. With keel hooks the fly has to be turned upside down to utilise the keel effect, but who's to say this isn't the right side up? For five centuries hooks have been getting stuck in weeds so something HAS to be wrong.'

That final comment expresses the keel hook's value in a nutshell. Haven't we all jibbed at covering fish because it was odds-on that we would hook greenstuff or bark before the fly was taken? And haven't we all acknowledged that a fish was good enough to warrant the risk, and paid the price? Now, snagging is virtually a thing of the past. Keel flies can be cast into bankside vegetation for the sheer joy of tweeking them through tough grass and scrub and watching them fall, like thistledown, to trout waiting below.

It's immaterial whether the pattern is a dry or wet fly, nymph, streamer or one of the lightweight 'bugs' creeping in over here. That keel keeps the hook pointing to the sky. Where the line goes the hook will almost certainly follow. Strictly speaking, more than one feature keeps the point clear of snags: 1. Its position relative to the eye of the hook. 2. The protection given by the materials used in dressing the fly. 3. The weighted keel. When normal flies fall between weed stems or grasses their extreme lightness prevents them from resisting the angler's pull on the line; the barb of the hook digs deep. Keel flies pivot against twig or stem and ride clear.

Sizes now on sale in the United States are 2, 4, 6, 8, 10, 12, 14 and 16, with a range of saltwater patterns from No. 6 up to 3/o's. Don't discount those sea feathers; they could prove useful even on mackerel traces in weed-thick water, and their snag-free quality could produce sport from grounds where normal spoons and feathers would be unfishable. Brain-child of Dick Pobst of Jackson, USA, the keel hook has a tremendous future. If close-up pictures are any guide, these flies look a little more natural than many we have used for generations. Nymphs look neither more nor less like the real thing to my eye, and with wet flies the hook is almost totally hidden. I'm told that dry flies float high, the hook point clear of the surface rather than projecting on to or below it. With streamers the entire hook is hidden from view.

The story of how Pobst came to develop this new-style hook is worth recording on this side of the Atlantic, for this is a slice of angling history. Perhaps the oddest thing of all, Dick Pobst was at that time no angler—just the father of a fishing-mad son whose only water was a weedy three-acre lake, the frustrations of which are all too familiar to need further comment from me.

Papa Pobst had heard about the weedless hooks used with spinning tackle. Why, he asked, couldn't his son use a weedless fly hook? The answer: there wasn't such a thing. Masochists all, fly-anglers have for years endured the agonies of snagging weeds and branches, bank growth, themselves, other people and poor dumb animals in great variety, in return for those rare moments when wind, wrist, light and eye combine to achieve the 'impossible'.

In 1967 Dick Pobst got to work, bending and twisting all manner of hooks. The short ones were too short, the long ones barely long enough. The Keel Fly he now markets has an abnormally long shank to give the perfect pattern. As a result, his son is catching fish where none could be caught before and a hook design that only the most hidebound will resist may soon be available to us. And for those who delight in writing about fly dressings there's a beanfeast ahead!

FISH WITH A PILOT'S LICENCE

Visit the Caribbean and the first thing you are likely to hear is a calypso band. Hungry? The first item you'll notice on a typical island menu may be flying-fish pie. Highly valued as food, flying-fish are taken around the islands and off the coast of California, the fishermen using lights to attract and net them.

In the seas off India a different technique lures the little flying-fish to its doom. There, fishermen tie bundles of twigs to handlines and pay the lines out behind their boats. To the fish, those bundles appear to be natural surface debris, ideal spawning sites for eggs that would otherwise sink to the bottom. As the fish gather round so the twigs are drawn over enormous dip-nets and at the appropriate moment dip-nets, twigs and flying-fish are lifted from the water.

At least sixty species of flying-fish exist in various tropical and sub-tropical waters. All of them are gregarious, often forming shoals of considerable size. Only two are freshwater species, one located in the rivers of West Africa, the other in South America.

Garfish and halfbeaks are related to these saltwater flyers and display some aerial ability as they leap and skitter across the surface. There is, too, the flying gurnard, its long pectoral fins making it a natural glider. Arthur Parrott, a New Zealand ichthyologist, points out that mullet often jump from the water for distances of 10 to 20 times their own length. He suggests that in the course of these prodigious leaps the stiff pectoral fins are spread wide to give balance and extra lift.

But let's concentrate on the main group—the Exocoetidae, ranging from 6-18 in. in length. Why do they fly? Not, it seems, in search of food. Their main diet consists of crustaceans and miniature fishes, although anglers in the warmer reaches of the Gulf Stream have caught them on small flies. Clay pigeon enthusiasts, shooting from boats, manage to bag a fair number with small-bore shotguns. Having well-developed air bladders, the fish float after being shot and are easily collected.

The most likely explanation is that flight provides a means of escape from their enemies. At least it makes capture less certain, for the predators that really matter can move as fast as they can. To a flying-fish Public Enemy No. 1 is the dorado or dolphin-fish, which feeds extensively on this species. Sea birds also attack and slaughter large numbers.

There are two kinds of flying-fish—those with enlarged pectoral fins and those in which both pectoral and ventral fins are much enlarged, the latter having as it were a double set of 'wings'. In both types the lower part of the tail is elongated and noticeably larger than the upper lobe, giving extra propulsion and control as the fish taxis along before take-off. N. B. Marshall of the British Museum, writing in *The Life of Fishes*, estimates that immediately before a fish leaps into the air its tail is beating or sculling from side to side at the incredible speed of 50 complete movements a second.

McClane's *Encyclopaedia of Fishing* gives this admirable

description of flight in an American species, *Cypselurus califor-nicus* ... 'Before taking off *Cypselurus* swims just below the surface for some distance, its upper tail lobe often breaking the surface; then it turns upward and spreads its pectoral fins, leaving the water except for the lower lobe of its tail. Now vigorously beating its tail back and forth in a sculling motion, it taxis across the surface to gain flying speed. Finally, it extends its ventral fins and rises into the air. At the end of a flight a fish may close its wings and dive gracefully into the water, or it may plop down with a splash.'

Do they really fly, using their fins as a bird uses its wings? High-speed photography has revealed that the saltwater species do not. They glide through the air at about 35 m.p.h. with their pectoral fins held rigid. But the little freshwater species flap their fins with a rapid and very distinctive wing movement. Flight may extend over 1,000 ft. or more in the case of sea-based flying-fish, but is usually in the 100-300 ft. range and no more than 4-5 ft. above the water, except in a strong wind. There are records of flying-fish reaching higher than 30 ft. and at least one sighting in which the fish was airborne for 42 seconds as against the normal 10 seconds or less.

So much for these fish of blue seas and tropical sunshine; a change, perhaps, from roach, chub and pike. If flying-fish could survive in our climate would they add to the attractions of angling in the UK? I wonder.

THE PERCH OF POULAPHOUCA

The Poulaphouca affair began seriously enough. It ended after five of the gayest and most hilarious weeks in the history of Irish angling. The Electricity Supply Board started the ball rolling when, in 1951, they made the Dublin Trout Anglers' Association responsible for Poulaphouca Lake, 17 miles from the capital. Situated in the Wicklow Mountains, this artificially created reservoir has a bank-line 35 miles long, covers approximately nine square miles and holds water up to 70 ft. deep: quite a lake for anyone to manage.

As far as the trout fishermen were concerned, it had one grave disadvantage—perch. Poulaphouca housed perch in their tens of thousands, so much so that other plans to improve the fishery were just pie in the sky until someone found a means of eliminating or at least reducing the perch stocks to reasonable proportions.

Large-scale netting would have been hazardous and costly; trapping could remove only token numbers. The problem seemed insurmountable until the Association's treasurer, H. F. Yardley, master-minded a scheme that was to set the Irish Press alight and send anglers from far afield trekking towards the Wicklow Mountains.

The plan was simplicity itself. The Association would tag 100 perch and replace them at various points around the lake. Every tagged fish would qualify for an on-the-spot payment of £10; all fish to be retained and the angler whose tag coincided with a duplicate locked in the strong room of a Dublin bank to receive a further £90 in cash. The Dublin Trout Anglers' total liability was £1,090, a sum they did not possess but hoped to raise from the sale of day tickets at 3s apiece. In this, at least, the Gods were with them.

Yardley was a craftsman. If anyone thought to counterfeit the Association's tags they would work hard for their money. To begin with, they would need a supply of walrus tusk, the material from which he fashioned the delicate markers, each with a secret cipher carved into its design.

The contest was scheduled to start on Sunday, May 11, 1952, At the end of April the Association's troubles began. William Gargan, DTAA secretary, joined Mr. Yardley in constructing a perch trap and placing it for the capture of fish to be tagged. The spirits guarding the Wicklow range obviously disapproved. The float marking the trap broke loose from its anchor rope. Dragging the lake produced nothing; the trap was abandoned. Netsmen were called in, only to have their nets torn to ribbons after landing seven small perch. Netting was abandoned.

Fresh traps were made and some fine fish captured. These were placed in milk cans and submerged to await the arrival some days later of Dr. Went, in charge of tagging. Perverse creatures that they are, the perch took exception to such close confinement and when lifted for Dr. Went's expert attention every one of them was dead. By now, time was running out.

Even the weather turned against the organisers. In storms and high winds Gargan and Yardley worked like Trojans, but the perch of Poulaphouca were no fools: they discovered how to get out as well as how to get into the traps laid for them. With only hours to spare, 100 fish were caught, tagged and returned to the water.

From the opening day the scheme's success was never in doubt. On foot and riding every conceivable kind of vehicle, Irish anglers flocked to the reservoir. Within seven days four of the tagged fish were caught. A kind of 'perch-mania' gripped the South Eastern counties. Mr. Gargan wrote later that, 'The sleepy village of Blessington, situated on the lakeside, woke that Sunday morning to see their one street a mass of anglers after tagged perch. Special buses were run, crammed with anglers and tackle, families and girl friends. Unfortunately, the buses did not all return. Many had to thumb lifts and some few had to foot it the 17 miles home.'

Blessington's pubs ran dry and the stock of day tickets was quickly exhausted, but the perch were removed in their thousands. One man caught 1,700 fish in five weeks, not a tagged specimen among them. For the village youngsters the affair was a riot. Not content with 100 wanted fish they tagged their own with shirt buttons—a private contest at 2d. a go and a one shilling prize for each fish landed—until an unsuspecting visitor netted a shirt-buttoned perch and insisted that the Dublin Trout Anglers' Association were making monkeys of them all! Shirt buttons or no, the contest grew. It reached proportions undreamed of by its originator. Extra bailiffs had to be engaged as anglers arrived by the coachload from distant parts of the Republic.

It couldn't last. Fences are expensive and meadow grass a valuable crop. So many dead perch had been dumped near the reservoir that the authorities feared pollution—a hazard for those occupants of Dublin's fair city whose one interest in water was drinking the stuff. After five weeks the Electricity Supply Board called a halt. To what extent the scheme succeeded in the long run I cannot say, but of one thing we may be sure: Ireland will never see its like again!

HOOPY LAKE

The Japanese—a people with whom we have much in common. Like them, we live on an overcrowded, heavily industrialised group of islands. Fishery interests play an important part in both economies. Angling, in all its forms, is a leading pastime. In Tokyo they even fish indoors, with bar service and soft lighting. In parts of Britain they're fishing now by the glow of street lamps. No doubt we shall soon catch up!

Last year a Japanese Fishing Mission visited Canada. During their stay in British Columbia the visitors took time off to fish for trout at a spot known as Hoopy Lake. Catches were good, which surprised no one since Hoopy Lake is noted for its game fish. But the procedure that followed attracted much attention. Each angler wiped the slime from his best fish, painted one side with ink, pressed a sheet of rice paper against the carcase and pulled away a near-perfect imprint as a record of the day's sport. The ink was then washed off and the trout sent to be cooked.

It seems that the imprinting of sporting fish is a common practice in Japan. The result is not, of course, photographic, but the detail is remarkably clear and when nicely framed these prints make excellent wall decoration. Should the first impression prove unsatisfactory the angler has only to re-ink his fish, take a fresh sheet of paper and start again.

Unlike photography, exaggeration and downright trickery

are impossible—well, almost!—for these pictures cannot be other than life size. A record of the venue and date is inscribed on each sheet. The title reproduced here is from one of the prints taken by the North Japan-Canada Fishing Mission. For the benefit of those readers who failed 'O' level Japanese, it reads, 'Rainbow trout: Hoopy Lake: 3rd July 1965'.

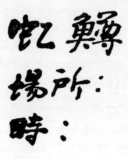

FIG. 2   Japanese title of fish imprint

MONSTERS ON A TROUT ROD

A visitor to Britain scanning the current crop of angling magazines could be excused the thought that in this country there is only one water where fly-fishing is even remotely worth while. But there are other places than Grafham—other reservoirs, for example. And we have splendid rivers and streams in the most charming settings. We have lochs and lakes and hill burns that make your fingers itch for the feel of a rod. And there's the sea. Fly-fishing at sea: now there's a thought!

Don't tell me that Old Tom has been at it for years, catching mullet in Christchurch Harbour, or that every summer Ivor Whatsit follows the mackerel shoals with his poor dead father's trout rod. I know these pioneers exist—a tiny nucleus of British saltwater anglers using standard fly tackle. We hear too little about their adventures and techniques, and they are, of course, very much a minority.

But in the USA thousands of anglers are turning to this relatively new branch of the sport. The Salt Water Fly Rodders of America have already taken shark to 270 lb., marlin to 150 lb., plus tarpon and dolphin, barracuda, tuna and bonefish, sailfish and striped bass on fly rods and lines that put the Grafham ballyhoo into something like its true perspective.

So what's wrong with trying for bass, mackerel, pollack, gar-fish, blue shark, porbeagles and a few other species, using the same techniques? Here's virgin territory for those sporting types who rate sea fishing gear as block and hawser tackle. But first, let's get up to date with developments overseas.

In the spring of 1966 the SWFROA announced that in future they would maintain official records for saltwater catches taken on fly tackle. They defined four separate classes, each governed by the maximum strength of the nylon leader connecting the fly line and the fly itself. These are ... FLY LIGHT, using leaders tapering to 6 lb. breaking strain. FLY MEDIUM, with leaders to 10 lb. b.s. FLY LIGHT-HEAVY, with leaders to 12 lb. b.s., and FLY HEAVY, with leaders to 15 lb. b.s. In order to qualify, each nylon leader must have a 12 in. length of the stipulated breaking strain. The usual thing is to tie the streamer flies to a 'shock section' of 80-100 lb. nylon and connect this with the tapered leader.

According to *Outdoor Life*, the average saltwater fly rod is 'a medium-action stick of 8½ to 9½ ft., weighing 5 to 7 ozs. It has to be a strong rod, and the man who uses it must have a strong arm. Tossing heavy streamers into the wind that usually prevails over large stretches of open water can be extremely tiring.' The reel and rod fittings—rings, reel seating and ferrules —must be resistant to saltwater, and the reel large enough to hold both the fly line and several hundred yards of backing. A favourite combination is a weight forward line, tapered leaders averaging 5-6 ft., and a backing of 250 yards of 27 lb. dacron.

Hundreds of American anglers have landed trophy fish with this type of outfit, but since my space is limited let me recount what happened when one of the finest anglers in the world—salmon expert Lee Wulff—took it into his head to meet the latest fly rod challenge. He planned to hook, play and boat a striped marlin on a single-handed 5½ oz. fly rod, a nine-footer, with a 4 in. diameter reel holding a 30 yd. fly line and 400 yds. of 17 lb. nylon. But there was one vital stipulation: every bit of this tackle was to consist of ordinary freshwater gear.

Wulff used a leader of only 12 lb. nylon and presented a two-hook streamer fly about 6 in. long, tied on 4/0 hooks and a short length of 100 lb. test monofilament. His first fish, contacted from a 15 ft. motorboat, was a 145 lb. marlin that battled its captor and itself almost to a standstill and was finally boated after four and a half hours.

No doubt many European skippers are already familiar with the technique used to bring game fish within range of the fly-rodder. Teaser baits, without hooks, are trolled from a sea rod set at the stern of the fast, open boats. The moment a fish is seen to be interested the teaser is wound in, drawing the fish closer; the engine is cut back and the streamer fly cast to the waiting fish.

This drill was evolved by the late Dr. Webster Robinson of Key West, whose captures with regulation fly tackle included a striped marlin weighing 146 lb. I believe that the largest game fish ever taken to SWFROA standards was the 151 lb. tarpon caught by 36-year-old Stu Apte off Miami. In 18 action-packed minutes Stu brought his fish alongside on a 30 lb. leader with the official 12 lb. section tied in. Backing? Two hundred yards of 20 lb. nylon.

Obviously, we do not have the same scope for big-game fishing as our counterparts in the warm waters of Florida and Panama, but some truly great little sportfish visit these shores each summer. They may be tiddlers by comparison with those in other parts of the world, but if it's sport you want with your shooting heads, streamers and heavy-duty tackle, why bother to line up at a reservoir?

No. 1 FISH HOSPITAL

On the shores of Toba Bay stands an ultra-modern building, hexagonal in design. Large Japanese symbols dominate one section of its outer walls; beneath them, in small lettering, is the English translation—FISH HOSPITAL. The hospital was established in 1965 as an adjunct to the famous Toba Aquarium housing up to 300 species and an estimated total of 4,000 saltwater fish, porpoises and sea turtles.

Curator of the hospital and its laboratories is Dr. Teruo Kataoka, concerned not only with the fish under treatment in the many hundreds of tanks, but with a postal service issuing prescriptions and advice to amateur and professional fish breeders in many parts of Japan. Dr. Kataoka works with a staff of eight specialists whose aim is to pinpoint curative treatment for the major fish diseases. Much of their research is based on drugs and chemicals administered to patients by our own G.Ps. Penicillin, for example, is prescribed in certain cases. Commercially-produced eye lotion, diluted in the water in which the fish live, has been shown to control 'pop eye' disease.

Fish farming will benefit greatly from this work, and through it the millions of people whose diet is below subsistence level. Angling, too, may benefit directly. I notice from the reports now available that research is at present concentrated on the bacteria giving rise to diseases such as pseudomonas, isolated together with columnaris and aeromonas by Dr. Margaret Brown and Dr. Collins in their early investigations into the disease we now term UDN. Much of the data we need in our own fisheries could eventually come from this remarkable establishment on the far edge of the Pacific Ocean.

LANDLOCKED: EXPERIMENTS
WE SHOULD TRY

Across the world are many examples of sea-going species that have been cut off from their normal migration routes, but which survive in circumstances foreign to most fish of their kind. The original powans of Loch Lomond and Loch Esk, and the vendace of Cumberland and Lochmaben, no doubt travelled considerable distances. Left behind when the waters of the Ice Age receded, they established themselves in these deepwater lakes and have thrived ever since. Neither powan nor vendace have much to recommend them to the angler, but several landlocked species give sport of the highest quality.

Certain waters in the United States, Canada, Argentina and New Zealand hold strains of Atlantic salmon that have not tasted saltwater for many generations. These 'landlocks', structurally the same as their sea-going cousins, but varying in colour according to the type of water and the lakebeds above which they spend their lives, have been caught on rod and line at weights up to 22½ lb. For the most part they are found in very large lakes and follow a migratory pattern around these fisheries. They spawn successfully in aerated water near inlet streams and lake outfalls, or on swift-water shallows with gravel bottoms.

In Finland there is a more primitive type of landlocked salmon, a fish seldom exceeding 6 lb. and averaging around the 2 lb. mark. Experiments still under way in the USA suggest that the striped bass will readily adapt to freshwater conditions and that it establishes and reproduces itself without difficulty in many large reservoirs. No coarse angler could wish for a finer fish.

Mullet are unlikely to breed when sealed off from the sea, but they grow at a fantastic pace. Australian mullet, trapped in freshwater 100 miles from the salt when Glenbawn Dam was built in New South Wales, reached weights more than twice the norm. The heaviest fish recorded from that area scaled nearly 15½ lb. I have long been convinced that angling clubs with lakes near the coast could have fine sport if only they would transfer limited numbers of mullet during the summer months. It's a fish many anglers scorn. I can only conclude that they have never caught one, for although most angling books suggest roach tackle and soft hookbaits, mullet will take fly and surprisingly large spinners, and they'll reject a treble hook in a split second after hitting it with such force that the rod tip bends hard over.

The most unlikely of all landlocked species is the common cod. At Lake Ogac, north of Labrador and on the shore of Frobisher Bay, landlocked cod have existed for thousands of years, and the only food they have available is themselves! Those that survive to attain seniority grow to a massive 40-50 lb. each. One expedition studying these fish caught a king-size 56-pounder almost five feet long. They really are cannibals, and always hungry. The only outlet from the lake is a tiny river that runs to the sea over a steep waterfall, and that fall is the key to the situation. Frobisher Bay has tides among the highest in the world; spring tides reverse the flow, climb level with the top of the fall and provide the cod with fresh supplies of saltwater. As a result, the surface layers of this strange fishery—the word Ogac is Eskimo for 'cod'—are 100 per cent freshwater. Incoming tides settle in the lower layers and here the cod exist in their hundreds.

Not for a moment would I suggest that we stock cod at Grafham and other big-water reservoirs, but as anglers overseas are proving, fish usually thought to be migratory can be utilised in fresh- and brackish-water sites. You may not agree, but I begin to feel that our polluted, mismanaged and sadly depleted stocks leave much to be desired by those who want lively fishing all the year round. The actions of Nature, and Man, in relation to these landlocked species is proof that there are many experiments we have yet to try.

PART TWO

FRESHWATER

HONOURS EVEN

I'm in bed with flu. The fact that five million people have had it and survived is no consolation. I know when I'm dying! In the corner of the room my rods are huddled in conference, protesting their inactivity and reminding me that I have yet to replace the stopper from the 7 ft. Spin-Gem—a stopper lost on my last visit to the Hampshire Avon. That was a crazy morning, if you like.

I had left my wife in the car, reading the Sunday papers, while I snatched two hours' fishing. I had sworn by every shrimp in the water that two hours would be the absolute limit—especially, I said, as it was pure chance that we had broken our journey at that particular spot. Dilly agreed. There was, she observed, the even greater coincidence that on a non-fishing trip my tackle should happen to be in the boot together with a can of lobs as fresh as any she had ever seen.

In the main river a big trout scorned all efforts with the freeline worm, and the pool below the sluice gates produced nothing. So I cut across country to take two nice chub, each topping the 2 lb. mark, from a heavily-weeded carrier. That water looked more inviting 200 yds. down, but to fish it I would have to cross to the other bank. Twenty minutes left. Was it worth it? A kingfisher flashed by—sure sign that all's right with the world. I sloped arms with the little cane rod and made through the autumn sunshine towards a crumbling, timber-built bridge.

As I recollect, that bridge is about 20 ft. long. Beneath it lay a deep, black hole, bordered by beds of wild cress so thick that at one point above the bridge they converged in mid-stream, almost shutting off the flow of water. I am sure there is an inner voice that warns all anglers when to be doubly alert, and

I was hearing it, right then. It was, of course, a likely spot for chub or perch, and a big trout could so easily have holed up under that jungle of weed. But the feeling I had involved something more than possibilities.

On my side, the bank close to the bridge was unfishable—a tangled mass of brambles sloping down to the mud, flags and weed growth. Cross the bridge quietly, I thought, then settle by those bushes on the far side. From there a lob could be cast easily and accurately. But you know what happens to the best laid plans. Half-way across I paused and peered cautiously over the handrail, making sure that my rod did not cut the skyline from below. Not a ripple disturbed that tiny pool, but for one brief moment I glimpsed movement many feet down ... Or did I?

I had opened the bail arm as I peered over. There had to be a fish in there! It was foolhardy, I know, but I could not resist the instinctive reaction to flick the rod and let the baited hook sail free. The worm fell with a gentle 'Plop!', wriggling as it sank slowly through the water, and all doubts disappeared as a chub rose from the depths, confident and unafraid, gliding to the bait now 18 in. or so below the surface. *Suck in: turn away.* At that point I tightened on him.

Three and a half pounds of well-muscled fish made for the cress beds like a mad buffalo, changed its mind and headed under the bridge with a rush that carried it to the other side. Angler and rod doubled in two in an effort to apply maximum pressure to the 4 lb. line and keep the nylon clear of the bridge timbers. Somehow I got him back to the pool, with enough fight left for three fish, and as I looked round to decide my next move, he dived. Hold it, fellah! I began to wish I hadn't started this at all. He bored deep again. It was then that I made the wrong decision.

I'd move back to the end of the bridge, drop down through the brambles on to the mud and weed, and play him from there. It seemed a reasonable manoeuvre.

In the event it proved almost disastrous. At the end of the bridge, holding Clarence on a tight line, I dropped the 6 ft. or so to the deck—only to find there was no deck there at all. There was no soil, no mud. There was nothing against that bridge upright but a deceptive tangle of blackberry vines and a mat of water weeds that had me completely fooled. I went straight through!

That was the only fish I ever played while suffering from shock and up to my midriff in water. But I got him and lifted the hook clear. It was a minute or two before either of us had enough puff to get going again, and as he nosed out into the pool I was chattering with cold. 'Let's c-call it a d-draw,' I said, and with that forced my way to the bank and sloshed back to wife and car. Oddly enough, I didn't even catch cold, but I have a real stinker at the moment. Thank heaven for fishing memories ... Negst tibe I shall loog bevore I leap!

SIGHT OR SENSITIVITY?

Most anglers will agree that by tracking upstream they can get closer to their quarry, without being detected, than they can by fishing downstream. They will tell you that this is due to the blind area in the fish's field of vision—a narrow strip immediately behind and above the fish in which it can see nothing at all.

I do not dispute that this blind area exists or that the approach from behind is more effective, but I do quarrel with the belief that the two facts are necessarily connected.

Watch a single fish—a trout, perhaps—resting in a clear-water stream on a hot summer day. It is rarely still for long. It needs but the slightest movement to tilt its window of vision to left or right. And as it moves, almost imperceptibly, so the blind area varies and the entire scene within its range of vision is kept in check. When tracking a shoal of fish the blind area is virtually non-existent as a factor favouring the angler. Each

fish lies at a slightly different angle to the stream; the blind
area, while varying from one individual to another, does not
exist within the shoal's total range of vision. They move as a
group. Scare one, scare all!

Even so, it is still easier to track upstream than down. Why,
if the 'blind spot/upstream approach' theory is a fallacy? I
suggest that vibration plays a far greater part than vision.

All fish have a unique extra-sense controlled by the lateral
nerve. Most of us are familiar with the function of the lateral
lines running the full length of the fish's body. Described by
many writers as being 'half-way between hearing and feeling',
this strange and fishy sense is used to detect obstructions and
low-frequency vibrations beneath the surface. It has a more
direct bearing on the well-being of fish than touch, taste, smell
or even sight itself. If that surprises you I suggest it's a typically
human reaction. We assume too easily that a sense we cannot
experience can hardly matter more than those we prize so
highly.

Experiments by Dr. Theodore Walker at the Scripps Institution of Oceanography, California, indicate that the lateral system
is the master sense without which life under water would be
impossible. Knowing that blind fish can feed, avoid obstructions,
sense and avoid danger, and even maintain position in a shoal
swimming in formation, Dr. Walker set out to demonstrate the
influence of the lateral line nerve system and its importance in
relation to other senses.

This super-sensitive nerve system is not confined to the line
visible on each side of the body. Indeed, these lines or nerve
channels play a relatively minor role in some species. The head
is networked with nerve extensions connected to the lateral
canal and so to the brain—a frontal system highly developed
in pike and chub. Parts of a pike's head are dotted with fluid-
bearing pores which react to the slightest vibration or change
of pressure.

At the Scripps Institution a school of fish was housed in an
aquarium. It was a simple matter to show how they panicked
and darted away when the demonstrator placed his finger in the

water. They didn't have to be looking at him: at such close quarters the lateral system responded immediately to the vibrations set up. But when the heads of those same fish were covered with thin latex rubber hoods—'cut outs' allowing the pectoral fins, gills, mouth and eyes to function normally—a very different situation was seen to exist.

The fish could no longer detect the approach of foreign objects, and allowed Dr. Walker to handle them and push them around as he pleased. The fully exposed lateral line failed to convey danger signals and a hand, clearly visible in the water, caused no apparent alarm. Not only did the entire lateral system cease to function when the head was covered, but neither sight nor any other sense seemed able to compensate.

The conclusion to be drawn is that while a fish can function, often reasonably well, without one or more of the senses shared with Man, it has little chance of survival if its lateral nerves are adversely affected. That much we knew or could have guessed. What few anglers may have realised is that, in some species at least, the essential control area appears to be concentrated on the surface of the head rather than the more obvious lateral lines of the body, important though these may be.

Consider this in relation to an angler fishing downstream. Any vibration he sets up makes maximum impact on the lateral nerve system at its most sensitive point—the head of the fish, facing upstream. (Fig. 3a.) A chub, for example, hovers in the current like a miniature Jodrell Bank telescope, its lateral nerves providing a superb early-warning system.

An approach from behind, from downstream, gives the angler definite advantages, not least that the fish's network of detectors is directed mainly away from him and is, in any case, partly shielded by the tail and shoulders. (Fig. 3b.) Sensitivity is decreased. Of course there will be reaction if the vibrations from downstream are powerful enough. But all things being equal, the effect of such vibrations must be weaker since the frontal nerve system faces away from the source and is to some extent tuned to movement, pressure and counter-vibrations coming from the opposite direction.

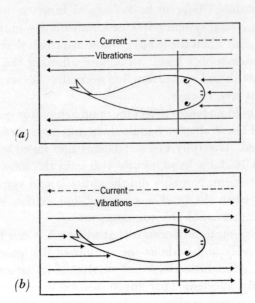

FIG. 3   *Sight or sensitivity? (a) fishing downstream. (b) fishing upstream*

With the upstream approach, the main warning system is reduced to minimum efficiency. This much seems clear, although it may be more true of some species than others. I suggest it is this, and not the alleged flaws in the fish's vision, that creates advantages for the angler. And if this is so, the theory we have honoured for many years becomes at best a half-truth—one more candidate for the boneyard of angling facts proved, in the light of modern research and analysis, to be so many fallacies!

PLAY YOUR HUNCHES

'Let's go fishing!' It was Pat Armstrong on the phone. Weekend or no weekend, he knew how much work I had to get through—

Pat was my Features Editor at that time. But a rowboat on the Thames was not to be dismissed so lightly. When he rang the front door bell, 20 minutes later, I was ready.

Long rods and two men in a boat are not the happiest of combinations. When Pat put the phone down I left my 12-footer in the rack and grabbed a 7 ft. spinning rod with a test curve of 1 lb. 2 oz., a neat maid-of-all-work that has given valiant service when legering, freelining, livebaiting and spinning. Which goes to show that the perfectionists who insist on rods of a certain length for every job in the angling calendar may be knowledgeable and perhaps wealthy, but they lack versatility.

We moored the boat to one side of the weir; sent lobworms and single swan shots on a whirligig journey wherever the current had a fancy to carry them. Ten feet away, a willow shaded part of the pool. 'I wonder,' said Pat, tearing a bread crust in half. 'I wonder if any chub are lying in there.' He threw one piece and watched it drift downstream. Then the other. Then, wham! As the bread touched the water there was a sullen swirl and it disappeared. Pike! A playful and obviously hungry jack pike.

Pat reached for a hypodermic, wound in his tackle and quickly removed the lead. He pressed air into one end of his bait, swung it over the side and let it float past the willow. Nothing doing! Again he tried, casting the weightless worm close under the tree. This time, as it splashed down on the surface film, the water boiled and a handsome jack was giving its would-be captor plenty to do. What great sport these fish are on the right tackle.

For the rest of that morning we tried various tactics from several vantage points. Not a fish; not a bite. It was nearly 2 o'clock when we moved the boat through a narrow inlet connecting with a small backwater. What a pleasure it was to escape the small powerboats and the noise of the weir; to glide into a spot truly wild and yet so close to the hustling life of the Thames. It seemed almost unreal, but the bright yellow water lilies, the rushes and the purple loosestrife gracing its banks— even the half-dead trees which have fallen and blocked the far end—are all fed by water from the main weirpool.

As a fishing spot, it looked good. Small fry were plentiful and the lily leaves thick with snails. There was shelter and food for a whole army of roach. But no fish, or so it seemed. Three hours later we moved back to the weir to find that of the four other boats in the pool only one had caught anything—another small pike. We fished hard until 8 o'clock that evening, but strong sunlight and a SE wind made bad medicine, and all the optimism we could muster—you know the sort of thing: 'They'll be feeding any time now!'—just didn't ring true.

'Well,' said Pat, 'I'm not proud. I'm going pimping.' So saying, he switched to maggot, float and a No. 16. Within 15 minutes he had seven bleak in the can; seven very useful livebaits had we wanted to fish that way. But for some reason I cannot define, I had an urge to return to that backwater. It was illogical, a hunch, but return I must.

As we drifted into position, the sun low and a mass of fly life on the water, that spot looked good for anything. Perch, roach, bream, pike—all could have been moving beneath the clear, calm surface. Pat baited with crust. I chose half-lobs, heavy enough to reach the lilies on the far side. The baits sank; our lines followed more slowly, leaving an unmistakable bow from the surface to the tip of each rod.

Minutes later my line twitched, urgently. Then it cut slowly through the water and as it tightened I lifted the rod and struck firmly into the last fish I would expect to find on the edge of a Thames weir. Solid, black-finned and covering the net with a blue slime, was a 1½ lb. tench. When we packed up an hour later I'd netted five and Pat two more—a bag of tench up to 2½ lb. on what had promised to be an almost blank day. Days like this produce the most pleasant memories. It was dark, quite dark, as we rowed the old boat down through the weirpool, muttering joyfully about sticking it out, playing one's hunches and still having a pile of work to do!

TIDDLER TOPICS

Few European waters are without minnows. You'll find them in rivers on the lowland plains, in alpine pools 6,500 ft. above sea level. Only in Iceland, southern Spain and the tip of Italy are they virtually unknown. I make no apology for devoting an entire article to this little fish. Sure, it's a fine bait for perch and chub, be it alive or dead, and you may wonder that there is anything more to be said. But hunting fish, like tracking game with a camera, is the more enjoyable if one has some knowledge of the many species encountered from time to time.

Fortunately, a great deal is known about the minnow. Its small size, hardiness and adaptability provide research scientists with an ideal subject on which to test theories relating to larger species. It has, for example, a remarkable sense of smell. Not only does it use this sense to distinguish between other fish and its own kind; it can even recognise one minnow from another! As a prominent biologist has pointed out, in this respect *Phoxinus phoxinus* is the equal of any mammal.

Locating members of its own species by smell is part and parcel of the shoaling instinct, applicable in less or greater degree to roach, rudd and bream. To this day there are those who doubt whether fish can smell. Others acknowledge that they can, but ask, 'So what?' The minnow proves capable of detecting sugar in water at a level 100 times weaker than the average human can achieve. So what? The minnow is not alone in this respect. Everything points to the fact that food smells, bait smells, have some bearing on our day's sport.

Of many tests involving the minnow and its sense of smell, one is of special interest. Anglers have often debated the question of fear in fishes. Do they experience fear? Not as we know it, with all its psychological implications, but it has been established that when injured or dying, minnows—like most shoal

53

fish—release a skin substance that scientists describe as 'fear liquid'. Water tainted with this liquid has the effect of terrifying and scattering other fish of the same kind.

If you ever have the good fortune to spot a pike near a shoal of minnows, *freeze*, and watch what happens. The little fish to one side of the pike, and those approaching from behind, will often smell the enemy before they see it. Most of the shoal will scatter at maximum revs-per-minnow. Others become motionless and sink gently to the bottom. This complete lack of movement is an instinctive attempt to avoid setting up vibrations likely to react on the pike's lateral line.

Oddly enough, both pike and minnow have different lateral systems to most coarse fish in the UK. In each case, this vital nerve channel is partly exposed—not hidden under protective scaling. The minnow's takes the form of an open groove in which stand flexible 'radar aerials' that bend under water pressure and respond to vibrations to which the fish reacts immediately.

So sensitive is this warning system that relative to the minnow's size its lateral nerve is among the most delicate of all British species. Super-sensitive is perhaps a better term. If a water flea moves near a minnow's tail, even in pitch darkness, the fish will turn at speed and take it. To get this in its proper perspective let me add that the average water flea measures no more than .08 of an inch!

The colouring of minnows varies from one area to another, depending largely on the oxygen content of the water. There are, of course, variations within the species. One is the marsh minnow, *Phoxinus percunus*, which has a slightly deeper body, golden-brown colouring and a bold, dark stripe along its entire length, emphasising the lighter and much finer lateral line. Forget the so-called mud-minnow of Austria and Hungary. Averaging 3 in. in length this is strictly no minnow at all: its nearest relative is the pike!

In the spring both male and female assume the brighter colours and markings appropriate to the spawning period. If you set out to trap minnows during the close season you will have no difficulty in distinguishing between the sexes. The male is always darker and bears traces of red on the underparts. As to food under natural conditions, the minnow lives largely on minute animal life and tiny insects hatching below the surface or drifting on the water, but is not above scavenging on any fish carcases it may find.

Few anglers who fish for the pot give the teeming minnow shoals a second thought, yet this little fish is said to match the gudgeon as the main ingredient in a good fry-up. Minnow tansy was a favourite dish some centuries ago—minnows, egg yolk, cowslip or primrose petals, and a little tansy. But back to the rod: in many a gravel pit and stream, perch patrol just beyond the shallows, waiting for any small fry brash enough to wander too far afield. Anglers interested in these striped hunters will find that one bait beats all others. Whatever the conditions, it's the minnow!

FAR FROM LADYLIKE!

Some time ago Tag Barnes wrote about the possibility of catching grayling with a spinner. Stephen Crane had started the ball rolling by taking four fish weighing more than a pound each from the River Hull in East Yorkshire. Tag followed up, devoting the last 30 minutes of a blank day's pike fishing to this method. The result, a $1\frac{1}{2}$ lb. grayling in prime condition.

'I am beginning to suspect,' he wrote, 'that these fish are more predatory than one might think.' Others have reached the same conclusion. Oliver Kite made quite a thing of the 'induced take' —fly-fishing for grayling with a bare hook, or one weighted with a few twists of fuse wire to make it sink, using a typical sink-and-draw action to attract the fish. Whether his lure resembled nymph or fry as it flashed below-surface is debatable: only a grayling could answer that one.

In July I spent some happy days with Tom Williams, fishing

The Avon below Salisbury. The river was in flood, but as one
local man put it, 'We're luckier than the West Country fishermen. Our water still has banks!' It had, in parts.

Using bread paste and a 12 ft. roach rod, I took dace, grayling
and a couple of chub from an almost wintery-looking eddy, then
turned from the main river to explore shallow water flowing
behind a big island. It was just 5.30 p.m. The few flies on the
surface were being ignored, but there were dozens of grayling
along that stretch. It seemed the perfect opportunity to put the
'predatory fish' theory to the test.

I set up my 7 ft. fly-cum-spinning-rod, mounted a fixed spool
reel loaded with 3 lb. line, tied on one of the new ABU Droppens
—weight: 1/16th of an ounce—and began wading downstream.

If anyone wants to talk of ethics and sportsmanship on game
fishing waters, let me say at once that these spinners are so light
that the average wet-fly man can out-distance you every time.
And with a lure tipping the scale at something like one gram
you have to wade very carefully indeed if fish are to be kept
within reach. This is sportfishing at its most sensitive.

Even when the spinner is held stationary in a moderate current the rotating vane gives a most provocative flutter. And with
intelligent use of rod tip and reel handle the lure assumes a life
of its own. Throughout the retrieve it is *dart forward, fall back
slightly, pause and dart forward again.* And when a grayling
takes there is no mistaking the fact. When she's out to kill, the
Lady of the Stream is far from shy!

My bag was 15 fish, ranging from 4 oz. to a beauty topping
the 1½ lb. mark, in two short hours. Even at that early stage
of the season, they were in tip-top condition. I would have
been happy to continue, but the fish had other ideas. A hatch
of blue winged olives got under way and that was that. The
spinner, so successful only a few minutes before, produced nothing further. But a rapid change from fixed spool to dry fly
kept sport at fever pitch.

All through that week the story was the same. I lost count of
the number of grayling taken on spinner, but I learned a lot.
I learned the hard way that these lures are murderous weapons,

so tiny that any fish given to snapping up a flashy trifle engulfs
the entire treble and is invariably snagged on all three hooks.
Unhappily, my first fish did just that. I had no option but to
kill it; that vicious little hook had done its work only too
well.

Once was enough: I reached for the pliers and snapped two
points from every treble I was carrying. Is it too much to ask
the manufacturers to make this unnecessary in future? A single
hook is plenty on spinners no larger than a fly spoon.

As to grayling and other fish attacking these little 'flashers',
it is true that we have tended to stare wide-eyed at reports coming
in over the years. Tench, bream and dace were among those captures: the odd grayling also. But our amazement was under-
standable—the lures those fish went for were relatively large
ones. The miniatures now produced are tinier than anything
ever used before, and this, I think, is the key point. They are
so minute that even small-mouthed fish like dace can get to
grips with them quite easily. Any fish reacting to the flash of
nymph or fry will attack these Size o and Size 1 spinners with
confidence—they're too small to fight back!

ROACH RUDD AND BREAM
ON SPINNERS

The man who popularised the fixed-spool reel was Alexander
Wanless. Before the war he fought many a battle in the angling
Press, defending and extolling the virtues of what he termed the
'threadline reel'. In those days it was used with specially designed
and very slender rods, lines of minimum breaking strains, and
the lightest of lures.

The majority of British anglers have long-since forgotten how
versatile the fixed-spool reel can be. They use it because it casts
a float or leger lead farther, easier and more accurately than a
centre-pin model in inexperienced hands. They tend to ignore

its ability to cast a variety of baits, without floats, leads or any other encumbrance, and so keep disturbance of the water to a minimum. They forget that an efficient fixed-spool reel, loaded with line of 2 lb. breaking strain, can play a fish many times that poundage, safely and surely.

Let's turn to other matters. At first glance they have no connection with the principles of threadline fishing. I notice from time to time, as no doubt you do, letters and news items dealing with coarse fish captured on livebaits, deadbaits and spinners. In January, 1967, Mr. J. Rouse of Bristol reported a 1¼ lb. tench taken on a small, dead dace. In March that year Mr. R. G. Pleavin of Warrington lip-hooked a six-inch rudd while spinning for reservoir pike. Incidentally, his spinner was four inches long! Other reports refer to bream, roach and dace, all taken on spoons or small livebaits. There have been too many over the years for these catches to be classified as mere chance.

Many years ago, Bertram Dawson included the following note in an *Angler's News* article on roach fishing in 1900 ... 'A method when warm summer breezes ruffled the surface of the water was to use a 14 ft. or 16 ft. cane or bamboo rod, a three-yard cast of 7x and a No. 14 hook baited with a strip of bread-crust. This was cast out in the same manner as that used by the fly-fisherman and slowly drawn across or against the waves, when its brown and white colours oscillated and flashed alluringly just below the surface.' With this moving, twisting bait our fathers and grandfathers caught summer roach!

You may remember my own report in 1966 of the way in which Laurie Theobald of Epsom took roach from a shallow water by twitching the bait across the bed of the pond. Insects, small fry—whatever the roach assumed these baits to be, I am sure that in some waters the big fish need more to eat than silk-weed.

Another tit-bit of seemingly unconnected data. Goldfish have a hearty appetite for their own young. Unless a breeding pond has shallows to which the adult fish do not have access, few second generation goldfish will survive. The crucian carp is directly related, other fish less so.

In Canada and America we find light-tackle specialists taking carp and all manner of fish on miniature lures of feather, cork, wood and metal, using one-handed rods of 5-6 ft.—casting nearly weightless lures from small fixed-spool reels such as the dainty Mitchell 308 and landing good fish on 2 lb. line. A combination of the slipping-clutch and snag-free waters are obviously of value with such tackle. But the reel alone is not enough. The rods are designed, as British models like the old Milward Special once were, to fight the fish and give backing to the gossamer-like thread that holds it.

Nearer home we have dramatic evidence that we may indeed be missing out on some very interesting sport. One of the best-known of all Continental anglers is the Dutchman, Frans Domhof. I read an article of his some years ago claiming that in Holland they spin with lighter, finer tackle than elsewhere. His comment on non-predatory fish, roach and rudd in particular, made me sit up and take notice. For nearly 20 years now, Dutch anglers have set out to take big fish of these species on threadline spinning gear. They use rods 6-7 ft. long. Some are of fibreglass, but good split-cane is preferred, each weapon having the action of a dainty dry-fly rod.

With these superb little rods they cast trout fly spoons, tiny bar spoons and home-made lures weighing, at most, only a few drams. Distance is not the object. The aim is to achieve a slow, fluttering retrieve without fear of catching the bottom or of disturbing or outpacing the fish. The next time you bait a swim and have the fish well on, put aside your float tackle, tie on one of these spinners and give it a trial run.

THE CHUB QUEUED UP,
BUT NOT FOR ME!

Have you ever tried to analyse a blank day, or a good day's fishing for that matter? It's a useful exercise. The factors accounting for success or failure are subject to limitless permutations.

Pat Armstrong of *Angler's Mail* fished with me several times during the 1966-67 season. I remember that on one occasion he had a fine bag of fish and some very exciting sport in the last hour of daylight, but nothing until then. I ended the day with an adolescent chub taken—I regret to say—by the simple expedient of poaching Pat's swim. Of that, more later. It will suffice to show that I was desperate for fish, trying hard and getting nowhere.

It was quite dark when we packed our tackle. On the far bank a group of poplars stood like sentinels against the night sky, and although no one could call either of us *noisy* people, the stillness seemed to amplify every sound we made. Trudging back across the water meadows Pat paused for a moment to shift his rod case to the other shoulder. 'You know, John, if we'd caught fish in the first hour this could have been a magnificent day.' I pondered the logic of that remark, admitted myself beaten and asked, 'Why?'

'Because,' said Pat, 'neither of us would have started roving in the first place. Having got one fish we'd have used the same bait, the same technique and stayed in the same spot to take others.'

That made sense. Both the river and the weirpool we had fished earlier are known to hold a good head of chub, roach and dace—all shoal fish. Catch one and the chances are that others will follow. As it happened, the early part of the day had been a dead period. We moved, and I suppose we got into the habit of moving, wandering along the river and one of its feeder streams, trying various tactics without success. True, I hit into a good perch, a really big fellow, only to have it throw the hook just below the surface and leap into the air as stylishly as any American bass. I've never known that before. But there was nothing else.

In mid-afternoon Pat selected a swim near a bend in the main river and decided to 'stay put' whatever happened. I roved on, rejoining him for that last hour of daylight. I should have known better, for this proved to be the old, old story. The static angler had time to study his swim, to note every snag and eddy, to make trial runs at different depths and have everything ready for action if the fish decided to come on feed. By contrast, the man with itchy feet took each stretch of water at face value, fished it for a brief period and moved on.

At his chosen swim Pat found the edge of the main stream curling back on itself and forming eddies above a deep hole. The water then moved on *upstream* close to the bank, before being drawn into the main current once more. No matter where he cast, Pat's float always returned to a small patch of dead water just two feet in front of his stool. He adjusted his float until the bait barely touched bottom. Then he waited, tossing in an occasional handful of soaked bread from his canvas bucket.

I returned from my travels in time to see him land his second roach, a lovely fish of 1 lb. 8 oz. His previous catch must have weighed about a pound and a quarter, and both fish had taken breadcrust. Then the chub looked in; not big ones—12 or 14 in. apiece. As fast as the bait sank into that square foot of water so the float went under. Chub? They must have been queuing up to sample the stuff!

Green-eyed and with fingers crossed I took up position six yards downstream and flicked a lobworm tail into the main hole. It might as well have been one of the fountains in Trafalgar Square. Not once did I feel the touch of a fish, nor see the line twitch or hesitate for a second as it traversed that turbulent water. Pat, meanwhile, was scooping them out—chub, roach, and a solitary dace as I recall—as though nothing could be simpler. And that, after nine hours' hard fishing, is a diabolical sight to a man on short ration.

At 5.55 p.m. precisely, with the light all-but gone, he hit into another magnificent roach, a fish very close to specimen grade. It was too much for me. Poaching or not, as Pat lifted his fish clear and on to the bank I flicked worm and swanshot upstream and beyond him, guessing that it would find bottom near the magic spot. It did just that. Within seconds the line ran taut and a fish was on. When I say that I could have written the words

'At last!' in letters of blood, my blood, you'll know just how I felt. What a joy—what a relief!—to feel a tight line again. It was no super-roach, but an undersized chub that saved me from a blank day. This was a case of being thankful for small mercies. If, like Pat, I had settled much earlier then I, too, could have enjoyed a real bonanza. I didn't. It is a fact, you know ... Some people never learn!

TRACK 'EM TAIL FIRST

THE VIEW OF A CENTURY AGO ... 'Fishing with the worm is not usually held in such high estimation as it deserves; a circumstance entirely owing to its being but very imperfectly understood. Fly-fishers are apt to sneer at worm-fishing as a thing so simple that anyone may succeed in it—their notions of it being that it is practised either when the waters are swollen after rain, or with a float and sinkers in some deep pool; and it is not surprising that with such ideas they should hold it in contempt.

'Worm-fishing is only worthy of the name of sport when practised in streams inhabited by wary trout, when they are low and clear. Under such circumstances it becomes a branch of the art which, to be pursued with success, requires the most intimate acquaintance with the habits of the trout, and the nicest powers of casting, and which in point of difficulty is only inferior to fly-fishing. As a lure for trout, worm unquestionably ranks next to artificial fly.' *The Practical Angler* by W. C. Stewart, first published in March, 1857.

July brought the first red-letter day to come my way for some time. My watch showed 10 minutes to mid-day as I picked up my seven-footer and checked the contents of my satchel. All present and correct: hooks, lead shot, forceps, scissors, spare spool, scales, small pliers and a bag of brandlings.

A-worming I would go. Fond as I am of fly-fishing, in high summer it is often so much wasted effort—the river gin-clear, no hatch of fly, a bright sun shining and the foliage guarding many a tree-shaded swim at its most luxurious. Successful trouting on a year-round basis demands more methods than one. The purists are entitled to their opinion, but it's my belief that at times the worm is as sporting as any other technique and more so than some.

I tracked cautiously upstream, not because of any false notion that this is ethically the right direction when fishing the worm, but because more fish will be spotted by going up-water than down. Frankly, I prefer to fish downstream where deep water is concerned. Line control is easier, the strike immediate and sure. Ninety per cent of all fish taken will be lip-hooked and that's important if undersized specimens are to be returned in a fit state to grow-on.

On this occasion I faced half a mile of shallows and holes, the water on my left as I made up-river. There were lots of fish about, but apart from a chub that scaled just over 3 lb., nothing to set the nerves tingling. Not one trout did I see looking remotely like the fish I wanted to take home. The holes yielded little of interest except a perch, a lovely fish that came to the net with its red fins gleaming in the sunlight, its dorsal erect and a look in its eye which said: 'And what the heck do you think you're doing?'

1.30 p.m. I stopped for lunch, and a pipe of Dutch tobacco— a heady, overpowering smoke in the confines of a house or flat, but absolutely marvellous by a sunlit river. Half the stretch had been covered without a sign of a good 'un, but my 'take home' fish was around here somewhere. Perhaps there would be a hatch of fly and trout feeding in earnest later in the day.

By ten minutes to three I was at the end of the water. The northern boundary—a small carrier stream—joined the Avon just four paces ahead and with only a yard or two to go I had to admit that even the worm was no good today. Then, through a gap in the reeds, I saw its head and shoulders. A four-pounder? It could be. Certainly a prince of a fish, lying doggo close to the bank in water no more than 18 in. deep.

He lay a few feet below the point where the carrier stream met and blended with the main river. From a trout's point of

view the spot was well-chosen. Below him the bankside cover
was so thick that one had no chance of tossing a worm upstream.
And a clump of bushes on marshy ground at the very entrance
to the carrier shielded him nicely from anyone with ideas of
dropping a bait on his nose from a yard upstream. Up or
down, one false cast and it would all be over!

To have passed that gap in the reeds would have been suicidal.
There was nothing for it but to fall back a few paces then cut
off to the right, heading towards the stream. If it proved too
deep to wade I would have to think again.

It wasn't. I edged across the carrier, making for the upstream
corner of its outflow into the Avon, on tip-toe part of the way
to avoid flooding my waders. And after a journey that raised
barely a ripple, but seemed to last an eternity, I had him in view
again. There he was, lying head-on, some yards below me. So far,
so good.

I checked the flow of water between us and flicked the worm
forward—a small brandling on a No. 12 hook, with a single BB
shot 8 in. above it. It pierced the surface five feet ahead of the
fish, sank and finally settled less than 2 ft. to his left. I looked
at it, he looked at it, and neither of us moved an inch. Then
he glided towards it and hung in the water, the worm under his
body. Suspicious? He may have been.

I was already so still as to be part of the scenery and my
heart sank as he headed away, upstream and across, to a weed
bed out in mid-river. But that fish was moving too slowly to be
seriously alarmed. I'd get him yet. At the weed bed he turned.
I lifted the worm an inch or two in the water—*Look, fellah,
look!*—and as it started to settle the big trout went for it. I hit
him on the run.

No fish ever tested the rod and its 3 lb. line so effectively. This
was no tame trout, hand-reared in stew ponds for release in
stillwater. Several times he almost made it to the weeds, only
to be turned and brought back to fight it out in that crystal-clear
arena. Twice I reached for the net slung over my shoulder and
twice he took off on a fair old run, the clutch singing merrily.
But after eight minutes I had him beside me, head above

PLATE 1 (*left*) Lymington skipper Brian Macnamara weighs a 15 lb. bull huss taken by the author during a tope-fishing trip off the Needles, Isle of Wight. PLATE 2 (*right*) Phil Shatford with a resident of the Grand Union Canal. A personal best, his eel weighed 3 lb. 12 oz.; was caught at 4.50 a.m. Efgeeco's king-size landing net in the background.

PLATE 3 Spinning for bass at Chapman's Pool, Dorset. A Mitchell 300 fixed-spool reel and an ABU rod—the Atlantic 433—make a spendid combination for saltwater spinning and light surfcasting.

PLATE 4 (*top*) Action on the Great Ouse Relief Channel as Bill Chilling-worth bends into a pike of 20 lb., plus. Basil Chilvers standing by with the landing net. PLATE 5 Another fish of the Relief Channel: an 8 lb. 9 oz. zander. Introduced to open waters by an official of the Great Ouse River Board, this species will eventually spread across-country—a potential threat to many coarse and game fisheries.

surface and the net in the water behind him. And as the net slipped under him, the rod still bent, the line parted an inch above the hook. It was as close as that!

3.15 p.m. I waded ashore, heart pounding with excitement and the perspiration running off me. It had taken nearly half an hour to get this far: the strategy had succeeded—just. He topped $3\frac{1}{2}$ lb., not a monster, but a nice fish, and his fight against that light tackle is something I shall remember for a long time to come. I sat for a while, re-lit my pipe, then packed up for the day. Enough is enough. The river had given the fish I wanted. (See Plate 6.)

SUICIDE TACTICS

For some years Peter Stone has hammered out the message: *Don't be afraid of weed growth.* Many of us would at one time have turned pale at the sight of a weed-laden swim. We would move on, hoping to find a nice clear patch to fish in. Today, we think less of it, recognising the weed jungle as an obvious refuge for the fish we seek.

This thinking is more or less universal. Where 'soft' weeds are concerned Stone's Law applies, but thickets of water lilies, their leaves shading roots and stems looking like a primeval boneyard, are another matter. Whatever Peter Stone writes about these formidable 'cabbage patches', the average angler doesn't want to know. Floats, leads, nylon and other items of terminal tackle cost enough as it is. Why, he asks, take risks when the odds are stacked against the man on the bank?

In this I think Mr. Average is wrong. By considering the logic of Peter Stone's advice in more detail, blank days can sometimes be avoided. All you need is the courage to stick your neck out for the first time.

As a case in point, let me quote from a recent outing with my own club—Odhams Press Angling Society. It was a fixture of no consequence to anyone outside the club: a coach laid on, a silver trophy at stake and about 40 of us paying into the kitty. First-prize money worked out at £1.4.0d. and the winner weighed-in the dismal total of 2 lb. 1 oz.

We were guests on a delightful tributary of the River Kennet. At no point is the water more than four yards wide. It was as low as it is ever likely to be and although coloured by rains of the previous two days the stream was still very sluggish. A friend and I chose a stretch broken by thick cabbage patches, one at least 20 yds. long filling all but a narrow channel flowing along the far bank. Understandably, we decided to fish a small pool in the snag-free water downstream of this lily bed.

With two-thirds of the day gone our keepnets were empty. The bush telegraph brought occasional visitors confirming that Bill Stanley had taken a tench one inch under the size limit and Mr. So-and-So had a small chub. Arthur Endersby had caught two roach in the first five minutes, after which he'd become the club's leading gudgeon fancier.

It looked certain to be one of *those* weigh-ins—fifteen anglers, each with a solitary fish, two at the most. The rest would be as waterlicked as I felt at that moment. Half-a-dozen go-ers could win the day, but that was the problem: where would one find half a dozen fish? They were not in the main stream, and the shallows were so shallow that an 8 oz. chub would have had to walk through on its pelvic fins. This left one possible hot-spot —the cabbage patches.

From the adjoining swim Peter Mackrill suggested that I was taking on more than I could chew. 'You can't fish in the middle of that lot. You are bound to snag with every other cast.' I could see his point, but with less than two hours to go the risk was worth taking.

I stripped off the float, float caps and leads, and tied on a No. 8 Goldspur anchored firmly to a choice lobworm. But I needed more weight to get the bait upstream and across and take it smartly through the lily stems to the bed of the stream. A swan shot, 6 in. from the hook, solved that problem. A handful of worms went in as an aperitif.

Five minutes later the line between rod tip and surface came to life and a river perch was on. It proved just, and only just, a go-er. Ten minutes more and another perch came to the net, then a very nice roach, and then a long wait for the next bite. That bite, and another later, I missed. A clump of poppies, two yards away, blushed and turned in the breeze.

It's not difficult to bring a medium-sized fish to the top and skate it across the surface, even in thick lilies. For one thing, the fish virtually acts as a hook guard. But when you strike and fail to connect, you do so at your peril. The barb moves only a few inches before setting itself in a huge stalk or root. You may then have no option but to break, so a hook link of less strength than the line has obvious advantages. And if break you must, at least be kind to your rod. Wind in all slack, reach forward and twist the line round your *padded* left hand: then smash.

I lost a couple of hooks, for what that mattered, in return for my three fish. The fourth came just before the final whistle. The bag could so easily have been the half dozen I was looking for; indeed, it should have been. Four small fish, all from a suicide swim, were nothing to write home about, but they were enough to win a club trophy and keep the flag of unorthodox tactics firmly at the masthead. It's a tactic I do not recommend for every trip of the season. Worth remembering, perhaps. In the right circumstances it's the sort of crazy fishing that could win a lot of matches!

NO TIME FOR CONTEMPLATION

Tired of roach fishing? Had enough of sitting still all day, of weighing-in just as the evening rise gets started? The chances are that within easy reach of your home there's a venue offering action-packed sport of a quality few people associate with coarse fishing. It may be a reservoir or gravel pit, a lake, canal or a quiet loop of the main river. Any water where perch go on the rampage in that magic hour before dark is a sportfishing centre.

There is no question of hoping the fish will move into your swim; no need for groundbaiting, and the rules relating to cover and stillness can often be disregarded. When the fish move in, so do you—for the most exciting sport coarse angling has to offer.

From June until early autumn, whenever conditions are right, the perch shoals make for the shallows as the sun sets. They harry the small fry, take flies from the surface and leap from the water to reach insects hovering above their domain. And conditions usually are right after a warm day with little or no breeze. They are right when the wind has a westerly bias, but seldom so when it blows from the north or the east. Of course there will be exceptions, in angling there always are, but by watching for these conditions the man whose fishing time is limited can enjoy fabulous sport, fresh air and exercise within the space of two or three hours at the most.

Forget about float and leger, leave your stool at home and don't bother to carry a keepnet. You are going to be on your feet, one minute casting to an action-spot on the left, then moving yards in the other direction as the perch signal their line of travel. Tackle? That's up to you, with the one proviso that a light rod ensures maximum pleasure. I use a little dual-purpose rod built for me by Constable of Bromley. For fly-fishing it's the neatest seven-footer imaginable, as perfectly matched with the most inexpensive of the Intrepid fly reels as it is with the Garcia-Mitchell Automatic. And it will punch a line as far as I ever want it to go. For ultra-light spinning, freelining with worm and even casting a float on occasions, it provides instant conversion by sliding the rings up the handle to partner a Mitchell 308.

If in the early evening there is no sign of movement on the water I'm content to wait awhile or sometimes to wander along to another part of the fishery. Here and there a perch will jump or dimple the surface. Cast to it a couple of times and move on. Suddenly, one section of the water will come alive, often far out from the bank. That's the starting signal. As a rule, it will not be long before those fish and others are raiding the shallows. Sink-and-draw tactics will certainly catch perch on these occasions.

A light spinning rod armed with 3-4 lb. nylon and a spoon, deadbait or tiny plug is a good combination. The all-important quality is casting ability—the knack of placing a lure exactly where you want it to be. The same rod with a cluster of maggots and a swan shot 9 in. from the hook can be just as effective, but if you are using lobs thread them well over the hook shank. Why? Because at times your bait will be subjected to heavy pressure. When you are half-way through a slow retrieve you'll realise that the perch have moved on. In this game you don't wait. Interrupt the action, get that lure out of the water and cast to where fish are actually rising.

For a fly fisherman this is sport *par excellence.* Any wet fly with a bit of flash makes an ideal lure—a Butcher, perhaps, an Alexandra or a Teal and Silver. Polystickles, and the far daintier perch fry fashioned by Ken Sinfoil of Weirwood, are excellent during this twilight period.

Whatever method you adopt, keep it simple. With fly tackle, for example, make ONE FLY ONLY the rule. The best of us can get tangled and in near-darkness a single hook at the end of a tapered cast is enough to contend with. Forget about droppers!

There are two advantages with this type of coarse fishing, in addition to those already mentioned. The first is that most of your perch will be neatly lip-hooked: very few have any chance to gorge the bait. The second, and I've noticed this again and again, is that the fish often stop feeding while there are still a few minutes of half-light left. When this happens there is no mistaking it. Where the surface was boiling over a wide area everything suddenly goes still. It is as if someone had called 'Time, Gentlemen!' And since the experienced sportfishing enthusiast travels light, he knows that those precious minutes allow just enough time to break down his gear, pack the oddments into his satchel and head for home.

THE GREAT TENCH MYSTERY

The Great Tench Mystery opened quietly enough. Angler R. Blaber of Willesden had planned a day's roach fishing on a private stretch of the Kennet. His uncle was with him. It was a Sunday: February 11, 1951. Neither angler could have guessed that their day's sport was to spark off a national controversy, win the major trophy of the year and lose the British record.

Sport that day was pleasant enough. It seems unlikely that either angler had much thought for tench, let alone the monster that eventually slid into the net. That fish weighed 12 lb. 8 oz. It was unquestionably a tench, fairly caught and witnessed by three experienced anglers, one of whom was Lt.-Col. Gordon-Watson. It was weighed on scales tested by Government officials.

Just one hour later, fishing from the same spot, Blaber struck into a second tench which he played unsuccessfully for 20 minutes. At no stage did he have this fish under control and its loss was inevitable, but judging by its tail, glimpsed at various stages of the fight, it matched the specimen already captured. Whatever stars govern an angler's life, those in Mr. Blaber's heaven shone brightly during that fabulous day's sport. The next day he entered his fish for the British record.

The record list was at that time controlled by *The Angler's News*. Acting strictly in accordance with their rules, Mr. Blaber had taken particulars from the witnesses, weighed his fish and returned it to the water. Captor and witnesses noted that it was heavy with spawn. Its stomach, they said, was distended 'almost to the size of a football'. On February 24, having checked with all concerned, *The Angler's News* announced this 12½ lb. tench as the new record.

Then the storm broke! Wherever anglers met THE tench was discussed. Many contended that such an extraordinary increase in size over the previous record was highly suspect. Could the fish have been a carp? On March 17 the Editor published a special article. 'In view of these doubts,' he wrote, 'we made further enquiries of the witnesses. Their statements, together with other factors, confirm our opinion that the fish was a tench and that it weighed 12½ lb.'

It was emphasised that there was no reason why a tench of these proportions should not be taken in British waters. On the Continent weights of 15 lb. are by no means rare and a fish of 17 lb. has been recorded. The paper went on to quote the Reverend E. C. Alston, captor of a 7 lb. tench and to this day holder of the rudd record. 'I used to see monster tench in Ring Mere,' said the reverend gentleman. 'Some were very big, from seven to ten pounds. The one I caught, a seven-pounder, was one of the smaller ones there."

In view of his experience with big fish, the paper had no hesitation in accepting Mr. Alston's judgement that he did see tench of 10 lb. or more. It seemed obvious, they said, that tench in this country can grow to at least 11 lb. without any additional weight being provided by spawn. The new record fish was fairly caught and they were fully satisfied. The record would stand.

On March 31 the paper published a reader's letter, voicing the suspicions of many anglers. February seemed a little too early for tench to be so noticeably in spawn; could its stomach have been distended by dropsy? The Editor made no comment. Two weeks later questions were raised about record fish being returned to the water. The Great Tench Mystery had far-reaching repercussions. It was the start of a wider discontent leading ultimately to complete revision of the rules governing British record fish. Again, *The Angler's News* made no reply.

Then came the bombshell! On July 28 the paper published its Notable Fish List for the 1950-51 season. Mr. Blaber was awarded the Freshwater Challenge Cup and replica. His tench was placed at the head of its class with Mr. Foode's 8½-pounder, taken from the Leicester Canal, in second place.

But one page of the awards featured an article titled THE

RECORD TENCH. It explained that although Mr. Blaber had won the trophy for the heaviest specimen caught that year, and although he had conformed to all the rules, the committee had now decided that his fish could not qualify for major honours. It was, they said, abnormal. Accordingly, the record passed to Mr. Foode.

A Chelmsford reader expressed the majority view in a subsequent letter to the Editor: 'A proved tench of 12 lb. 8 oz. is a record tench. Abnormal, it is true, as opposed to the normal weight of this species, but are not all we anglers living in hope of landing such abnormalities?' But those responsible for the awards had the last word, digging themselves still deeper into the mud of controversy. 'There seems little doubt,' read the editorial footnote replying to that letter, 'that it was a deformed or diseased fish.'

Natural giant, freak or diseased specimen? It could still have been a record-breaker. But the 12½-pounder was never captured nor seen again, nor was the giant with which it shared the water. The Great Tench Mystery remains unsolved.

EEL HUNT!

'The water that came up trumps last year,' wrote Jim Gibbinson in the National Anguilla Club's bulletin, 'was the Grand Union Canal.' It came up trumps again when Bob Church, Dr. Terence Coulson, Phil Shatford and I fished it on a warm but very wet night at the end of April.

Through much of that Saturday afternoon and evening we sat at Bob's home in Northampton, drinking innumerable cups of tea, studying trout flies and lures, and talking fishing: talking eels.

I'm not an eel man. The odd 'bootlace' has come my way, as they have to most leger enthusiasts, but the thought of deliberately fishing for big eels had never entered my head until Bob invited me to join him on April 27.

Politically, the eel specialists face tremendous problems. Most river authorities break out in a rash the moment close season eel fishing is mentioned. A typical reaction is that anglers will abuse any privilege permitted in this respect, using it as an excuse for coarse fishing during the fence period: so, they forbid angling for eels. For this decision to be in any sense logical, they should at one and the same time ban trout and salmon fishing. But they don't. As a result, the game-fish laddies catch more coarse fish than the entire Anguilla Club will ever see.

In the Welland and Nene area close season eel fishing is OK, but to minimise risk to coarse fish the Authority insists on a hook with at least a half-inch gape. And the Anguilla Club, honouring that proviso, fish with 1/0 hooks and never carry anything smaller.

I learned that in the search for specimen eels—fish that started life to the south of Bermuda, thousands of miles from these shores—the Club 'clocked' 11,000 man-hours last year and netted 198 fish for a final tally of 56 rod-hours for each specimen. Fifty-six rod hours per fish! The chances of catching one on that particular night seemed rather remote.

Our convoy sped through a rain-washed twilight towards the Grand Union Canal at a point not far from Northampton. As we parked the cars the heavens opened. Someone wound down his window and called . . . 'Bob, let's go back to your place and just *talk* fishing!' Damp, but cheerful, we picked our swims; Terry Coulson and I taking the towpath under the road bridge. The rain had nothing to do with it, or so we said. That old brickwork beneath the bridge looked a readymade hotspot, and the path there was bone dry.

The water temperature checked 58 deg.F. Air, 60 deg.F. By 9 p.m. all four of us were in action, using rods capable of holding big bass, carp or pike; reels loaded with 12 lb. lines and joined, in each case, by a small split ring or swivel to a supple trace of nylon-covered wire of 15 lb. breaking strain.

The 1/0 hooks were baited with bunches of lobworms, heavy enough to cast without leads.

The Anguilla hunters are well organised. Buzzer indicators allow them to sleep much of the night; plastic dustbins serve as keepnets, keeping the fish alive and well until the dawn light. Folding bed chairs and umbrellas built like marquees give maximum comfort and all the cover they need. Their guest pressed his silver-paper indicator on to the line, put a match to a night light in an old cocoa tin and prepared to do his primitive best. In the face of all that super-tackle, plus a 56-hour average per fish, he didn't rate his chances too highly.

Ninety minutes later the silver paper sprang to life and a run started. I snapped the bail arm shut and struck firmly into the first eel of the season and the very first I had ever caught by intent. It wasn't a specimen. It wasn't a bootlace, either, and for several minutes that fish gave a very good account of itself.

Terry Coulson netted it, cut the line joining the trace and lowered fish and trace into a dustbin half filled with water. Bob joined us, grinning broadly. 'You're the guest,' he said. 'We're supposed to catch the eels!'

The night passed, hilarious at times. Of course we discussed angling politics and many a serious facet of the sport, but never shall I forget Terry Coulson's graphic account of Charles Chaplin in the old silent film, *The Pawnbroker*. Space forbids more than a brief reference, but even now my stomach muscles ache at the thought of Terry, feet set at a quarter to three, doffing an imaginary bowler hat and sweeping the remnants of a battered alarm clock into it from the counter of the pawnbroker's shop—on the towpath of the Grand Union, in pouring rain, at 3.25 a.m.!

Crayfish proved a curse for Terry, nipping his baits to pieces and taking line, a foot or so at a time, while his buzzer reacted like a morse-tapper at a square dance. But the star of the occasion was carp specialist, Phil Shatford. At 4.50 a.m., Phil had a copybook run and for the next ten minutes he battled grimly with a splendid eel, a real specimen this time. Every inch of its sleek, streamlined body twisted and turned, meeting pressure with pressure, and as the rod bent hard over that powerful tail-fin spread like a canoe paddle.

The session was over all too soon. The rain stopped and a choir of larks headed skywards: another day had begun. We weighed both fish on the towpath by the road bridge. At 3 lb. 12 oz., Phil's eel topped his previous best, a 3 lb. 7 oz. fish caught two seasons before. Mine scaled 1 lb. 10 oz. Not much, but it was at least an eel.

As Dr. Coulson completed the Club records two familiar figures peered over the bridge—Fred Wagstaffe and Bob Reynolds. 'Thought you'd be here,' said Fred. 'We've been after eels farther down the Canal.' They'd had a blank night and on past returns could do the same for the next six or seven nights before contacting another rod-bender. But as any eel specialist will tell you, it's worth the effort. I wouldn't disagree for a moment, and with such splendid company I'm game for a second attempt at any date they care to set.

THE GOBIO GATHERERS' GUILD

During the course of the first British Angling Conference I asked a member of the National Association of Specimen Groups what his committee's reaction would be if a group of gudgeon hunters applied for affiliation. He gave his personal reaction without realising that I was far from serious or that I was listening joyfully to the tinkling of bells following this most gentle of leg-pulls. He gave it without a saying a word. He frowned.

He rubbed his chin, thoughtfully, for some time. Then and only then did he voice the opinion—a purely personal one, you understand—that such a move was unlikely to be welcomed by the Association.

This is interesting. As far as I know, the NASG has never announced that its activities are limited to fishes of a certain size. Indeed, I hope this is not so. Someone may take it into his head to start a National Association of Small-Specimen Specimen Groups, and that great big wheel of fragmented angling organisations will start spinning all over again.

I have always assumed that *all* species capable of providing sport with rod and line—certainly those eligible for British records—have the blessing of the NASG. The gudgeon, *gobio gobio*, qualifies on both counts. And as any well-read angler knows, its poor reputation among some sections of the fraternity is of recent vintage, by no means unanimous and quite inaccurate.

Frank Buckland, Her Majesty's Inspector of Salmon Fisheries in the 1880s, went on record with the thought that only two kinds of fishing are worth bothering about—salmon and gudgeon. With the right tackle both fish guarantee a fair day's sport. With the right chef both have flavour enough to compete with all the fancy fishes from overseas. Ask for a dish of gudgeon at any one of London's top-flight hotels and no one will look at you in blank amazement. You may have to pronounce it 'goozchon', but they will know what you mean. Ask for chub and you'll be shown the back door.

A comment from the NASG's Press Officer would, I think, be of value. When one man's sport is another's boredom what is the factor qualifying for NASG membership? If scientific know-how is the prime target, why remain ignorant of so important a species? I am tempted to declare the immediate formation of the Gobio Gatherers' Guild. But this will come of its own volition. In Rugeley, Staffs, there's a chap specialising in the breed, intent on breaking the record and learning a great deal more about this fine little fish and the part it plays in that teeming metropolis below the surface. Good luck to him!

FISH IN FASHION

It used to be carp. Now, I think, the fashion has changed. Every year, more and more anglers are hunting the pike, a fish that abounds in waters ranging from farm ponds to mighty rivers.

Where piking is permitted in the summer months fishing for jack with ultra-light tackle gives tremendous sport. The thought may horrify the purists who consider October 1 as the feast of St. Esox, but that disturbs me not a bit. Coarse angling is cursed with more purists than the dry-fly fraternity ever produced.

Peter Hancock's 40 lb. fish, and Clive Loveland's 39-pounder only one week later, were the highlights of the 1966-67 back-end. Their success will prompt still more anglers to 'have a go'. And if relatively few of them catch pike weighing more than a third of those breath-taking weights they will at least experience thrills that put many other forms of angling in the shade.

In this day and age the unorthodox is too often frowned upon. *Homo Sapiens*—man the wise—has a habit of digging himself into ruts, and anglers are no exception. Our tackle has to be just so, our techniques precisely as laid down by 'X' or 'Y' or 'Z'. Alternatives are unthinkable to all but the rebels.

As pike fishing flourishes, so I imagine, does the sale of herrings and sprats. Livebaits, spinners and plugs are also acceptable, but little else. Our slavish adherence to the ways of the big-fish hunters robs us of experience and fun that could at times achieve remarkable results. One exception is Brian Martin of Sheffield. He uses mackerel because this is, to his eye, the only bait readily available that resembles a small pike. Right or wrong, this original thinking recently produced a 21-pounder.

The plain fact is that pike are creatures of catholic taste. Thread a treble through the heel of an old shoe and somewhere in Britain there's a fool pike ready to attack it!

It was Maurice Ingham who suggested some years ago that lures imitating fish on which pike normally feed might prove a disadvantage, being likely to attract only hungry pike, fish actually hunting for food. (Come to think of it, this *must* be true of static baits!) By contrast, wrote Ingham, any bait behaving in an off-beat way, or looking as if it had no right whatever to be in the water, triggers an attack mechanism that stimulates even a well-fed specimen.

Around 1870 fly-fishing for pike was a favourite sport in Ireland. Gaudy flies, ever bigger than the largest salmon lures, were considered ideal. There was many an argument about whether the pike took them for small fry or the dragon flies of summertime. I doubt if *Esox* gave the matter quite so much thought! The famous Kenmure pike, a 72-pounder from Galloway, is said to have fallen to a fly. Mackerel feathers would almost certainly prove attractive, and why not? Most self-respecting pike will attack anything that swims, from wild duck to water rats. I've often wondered how strips of cured rabbit skin would fare. For that matter, today's simulated fur fabrics offer a wealth of materials, many of which can be bought quite cheaply by the piece.

The Americans have three species of pike. The largest of these, the muskellunge, is named after the Red Indian *mas kinonge*, meaning great pike. The musky is described in true Yankee style as 'fighting like a demon and as moody as a mental patient'. The variety of baits used for this and other U.S. predators includes feather lures and strips of chamois leather that writhe through the water like living things.

But the game that appeals to me is the old Irish technique already mentioned, wet fly fishing. If salmon, carp and monster trout can be landed, why not the king of freshwater fishes? The great advantage of fly tackle would be the ability to fish without weight and on a slow retrieve, so timed as to make any pike see red.

Salmon flies and similar creations could land many good fish, even when presented on standard coarse tackle. The lure might be cast with a single swan shot, floated into position on bread or flotsam of some kind, or fished on tackle using a variation of the salt-leger technique.

Pike fishing offers scope for homemade lures; lures costing next to nothing; lures that will take as many fish as any expensive, factory-made flasher. Old tins can be flattened and snipped into shape to provide giant wobbling spoons that would otherwise cost a fortune. Feathers, fur, plastic, wool and metal foil are the materials for pike-challenging 'baits' that Old Izaak would have envied. Unorthodox they may be, but when a rebel angler strikes into a good fish he experiences a very special sense of satisfaction!

TROUT FROM THE SEA

In recent years the pages of the angling Press have carried remarkably few references to sea-trout. In the modern idiom, this beautiful fish has seldom hit the charts and to many anglers is something of a mystery. For that matter, it is something of a mystery to those who spend their lives studying the behaviour of various species. What, for example, prompts one trout to head down-river and into the open sea while another, apparently identical, steadfastly refuses to leave home?

The natural trout of Great Britain were once thought to comprise many varieties, the sea-trout being listed as *Salmo alba*. Their modern classification as a single species, *Salmo trutta*, acknowledges that variation in colour and size is entirely dependent on the environment in which each strain breeds and develops.

Young sea-trout are identical to the brown trout with which they may share the water—the ultimate difference in bulk and body colour resulting from a life cycle involving river, sea and then a return to the river, on the one hand, and a life spent entirely in freshwater, on the other.

One never gets far in studies of this kind without encountering words little-used in the sport, but commonplace in scientific circles. 'Anadromous' is one. Like its cousin, the salmon, and like the sturgeon, the sea-trout is anadromous, which is to say that it's a freshwater fish spending part of its life at sea, but always returning to freshwater to spawn. It is a sea-run or anadromous brown trout.

While the physical sameness is indisputable, the mystery of the migratory urge remains. There seem to be two schools of thought. Some experts believe that when a river's trout population threatens to outstrip the food supply a proportion of the fish will automatically migrate to saltwater. Others think that the situation is governed by hereditary factors formed way back in time and spanning thousands of generations. In this case, if access to the sea is readily available, migration will take place regardless of food supplies in the home water.

As to the distances involved, some biologists are of the opinion that very few sea-trout move far beyond the coastal influences of their own river outlet. Others, disputing this theory, speak of journeys up to 100 miles distant. Both could be right, for this factor must vary according to conditions along the coast adjacent to each estuary or rivermouth.

The vital phase of the sea-trout's move to saltwater has rarely been better described than it was by William B. Currie in his book, *Game Fishing*, published in 1962 by Stanley Paul Ltd: 'It is only in the second year (occasionally the first, sometimes the third) that the great distinction between the sea-trout—the migrant—and the brown trout—the resident—is seen. The sea-trout parr begin to move down towards the sea, changing their colour as they do so, donning a silvery coat which almost obliterates the spots and bars which have marked the fish's side since infancy. In the sea pools of the river, brackish and fresh by turns, they feed heartily, moving up and down with the tide. This may continue for some time before the second great stage of the migration takes place.'

That second stage is, of course, the move into saltwater once the sea-trout's metabolism has adjusted to requirements very different from those of freshwater fish and which enable them to survive in water of maximum salt content. From then on we know little about their way of life until they return to spawn—the larger specimens often being confused with salmon as they are caught along the lower reaches of their home stream.

In a few rivers the first run from the sea occurs as early as April; in the Orkneys sea-trout first show in February, but for the most part sea-trout fishing and the warmth of summer or early autumn coincide. This homeward move, be it early or late in the season; sometimes a single run, often more, varies from one river to another.

The first flush of incoming trout invariably brings the really big ones that have made the journey several times before, plus a number of first-timers, known as whitlings. It is unwise to place too much faith in any one point of difference between large sea-trout and salmon of small or average size.

Certainly it is rare for salmon to feed once they enter freshwater, and by contrast, sea-trout do not lose their appetites. As Dr. J. C. Mottram put it: 'The microscopic examination of the scales is a very sure way of distinguishing a large sea-trout from a salmon. The sea-trout is certain to be several years old and to show several spawning marks, whereas a salmon of corresponding weight is, by comparison, a baby in years and unlikely to show any spawning marks.'

Of its fighting qualities, F. W. Holiday once wrote: 'Fly-fishing for big sea-trout offers more than any angler has a right to expect from his sport.' His opinion is one with which spinning enthusiasts and skilled manipulators of the wriggling worm will also agree.

In case anyone should mistake that reference to 'big sea-trout' with the need for a specimen hunter's approach, I quote Sir Edward Grey (1919): 'I prefer a good fresh-run sea-trout of 3-4 lb. on a single-handed rod and fine tackle to anything else.' Bridgett (1929): 'Even a little fellow of half a pound is a source of amazement, a fighter from start to finish, while one of 3 lb. or more is a conquest of which any angler has reason to be proud.'

If big fish are needed, 20-pounders are not unknown, while Russian and Polish anglers claim specimens in the 30-40 lb. class. Whether at home or abroad, if the chance to go in search of the anadromous brown trout should come your way, don't hesitate. With luck, and no small measure of skill, you will sample some of the finest fishing in the world.

PERCH PUZZLE

A two-pound perch lay gleaming in the sunlight of a drowsy August afternoon, bright-eyed, defiant, every nerve controlling its dorsal fin at Action Stations. I can see that fish as if it was still in my landing net. In fact, we parted company several years ago.

Perhaps you've had such a capture; one particular fish that recalls not only the venue, but the very atmosphere of the place. Whenever I think of that perch I hear the rustle of tall reeds, grey-green in the summer light; sense the warmth and stillness of the landscape, and every detail of the trees overhanging that favourite river of mine. A blackbird—raucous, alarmed—flies across-river from the copse behind me, and the sheen reflected from the surface dazzles the mind's eye. My perch, now back in the water, pauses to regain its composure before thrusting into that strange world of pebbles, trailing weed and gin-clear water.

Perch are a law unto themselves. I would guess that we know less about this species, and about its specimen-sized fish in particular, than we do of any other freshwater fish.

Most of the outstanding specimens reported in the angling Press—they are few and far between—are chance captures, which is hardly surprising. Hunting big perch is the most frustrating pastime ever devised. One week you'll see them patrolling the water for all the world as though they'd taken up permanent residence, but by the following Sunday it seems to hold nothing but 6 oz. fish and those big, striped monsters are not heard of again for months on end.

There is one difference between hunting big eels and big perch—the perch-fisher can at least see what he is doing. The heartbreaks are identical. I don't blame anyone for concentrating on pike, tench or some other species that produces fairly regular returns.

Just as the salmon disease is reproducing conditions said to have existed at the beginning of the century, so London's anglers may be involved in a similar crisis concerning perch in the Thames. Immediately prior to the 1914-18 war Thames perch almost disappeared. The situation was so bad during the inter-war years that LAA members were forbidden to fish for perch before August 1, a restriction that remained in force until shortly after the 1939-45 war. That late start to the Londoner's perch season may have given rise to the reference to 'fine perch and autumn leaves'. Be that as it may, I have yet to be convinced that perch feed better or fight better when the leaves are falling than they do at any other time of the year.

By the late 1940s the Thames fish were at full strength once more. I doubt if this is so today. Reliable reports indicate that the number of perch in the river, gravel pits and reservoirs has been drastically reduced. Losses in the reservoirs alone account not for hundreds, but for many thousands of fine perch. Eyewitnesses are so definite on this point that it is patently absurd for the Metropolitan Water Board to suggest that 'nothing out of the ordinary has been noted'. Not even a one-eyed water diviner could expect that piece of blarney to be accepted.

London's tap water is drawn, for the most part, from the Thames. Any disease or pollution affecting the reservoirs will have come from, or find its way back to, the river itself. But only one thing is certain about known casualties: very few of them float at the surface. The dead perch seem to sink straight to the bottom. In the river, the odd carcase may be noticed as it drifts downstream, but vast numbers could be swept away unseen.

Apart from eye-witness accounts at the reservoirs, a report

from Keith Elliott at Maidenhead supports the view that river perch are also involved. Where good-sized fish were once plentiful along that sector, Keith has not caught one for an entire season, and the best he has heard of in club matches in the Maidenhead area was a mere 1½-pounder.

Young perch, bait stealers unable to resist the match anglers' maggots, are less evident than they were a few seasons ago. Still more significant, gudgeon shoals show an unprecedented increase. And since gudgeon are the No. 1 forage fish for river perch, they must have bred undisturbed for some time. Having said that, I acknowledge that their increased numbers could result from some other factor entirely. The doubt remains.

A sport better organised than our own would have set up an inquiry, produced one or more interim reports and followed this with a final report summarising the known facts. Instead, we have to guess what is happening, accept a lower standard of sport in return for the money spent on Water Board licences, and hope for the best.

Despite comments to the contrary, big perch are not easy prey for the average angler: far from it. They are as fearful and pernickety as any fish that swim. With that in mind, let me close with a piece of advice from Tom Williams, Fishery Manager at Longford Castle.

Tom told how his coarse anglers insist that the Avon perch are less numerous than they used to be, and how they thumb through the record books to prove the point. 'Perch,' he wrote, 'are early spawners. They are gravid from the beginning of March and in almost every case the large bags quoted to me had been caught just before the season closed. Every one of them came from dead water on the edge of deep holes. As the water reaches its coldest point the perch collect into vast shoals as a prelude to spawning. It is then they are vulnerable to the quiet angler. With our present increase in fishermen it's a shortage of quiet anglers, not perch, that is being reflected in the record books.' On the Avon, perhaps. The Thames and the City's reservoirs is, I suspect, another matter entirely.

KING LOB

As I write it is nearly 11 o'clock at night and a fine, soft rain is falling. The dry spell is over. For the first time in weeks my red torch has been in action and dozens of big lobworms are in the box ready for a tench session tomorrow morning. I live in a flat, with no garden worth talking about, but there are extensive lawns around the main buildings. Even so, maintaining a supply of lobs is not without problems.

This very evening I was crouched low on one of the lawns, watching for the unmistakable gleam of a lobworm in search of fodder. 'Have you LOST something?' Worm hunting requires concentration and the question was so totally unexpected that I almost took off! The voice, vibrant with suspicion, came from a neighbour who had seen this apparition scanning the lawns with a RED light, decided to investigate and, if need be, 'have a go'.

But the problems of bait-hungry anglers are as nothing compared with those of New York's Bronx Zoo. Some years ago the zoo took delivery of two web-footed, fur-coated, egg-laying, young-suckling, duck-billed platypuses—Cecil and Penelope—shipped out from their native Australia. In captivity these mixed-up creatures exist on a diet of earthworms, egg-custard and crayfish. 'No problems there,' said the Zoo authorities when the new stock was first offered to them. 'How many worms do they need?' At that point their troubles began. The ration needed to maintain life and a gloss on those fur coats was 25,000 choice worms a month.

The worm farms of America could not possibly supply that number. In any case, the cost would have been prohibitive. Work it out at 3s. a dozen. The figure approaches £4,000 a year—for one course on the platypus menu! The alternative was to start breeding worms, fast. So the cellars under the lion house were converted into the world's largest worm farm, with an output that only just satisfied the ravenous appetites of Cecil and Penelope.

Pits were built of breeze block, about 6 ft. square, each filled with fresh soil to a depth of 18 in., topped with a 6 in. layer of elm leaves. The worms are bred in small boxes to ensure proper control of the egg cocoons. These hatch in about 18 days and the tiny wormlets are moved to the growing pens when three weeks old. The stock is fed on what a Zoo spokesman once described as 'a balanced worm diet'. Stale cake, pea pods, sour milk, eggshells, toast, ashes, corn meal, orange skins, rotten fruit (most important, but avoid whole apples), coffee grounds and newspaper. All this to keep a couple of Nature's misfits in top condition!

Edward Hinchliffe wrote about worm hunting in an earlier edition of *Angler's Mail*. He suggested wearing an old woollen glove on the 'grabbing hand'. A sound idea. By the time two or three lobs have been caught your fingers are slippery with worm varnish and from then on a firm grip is almost impossible. The alternative is to carry a piece of cloth on which to dry your fingers after each capture. But see to it that it hangs from your pocket before the hunt gets under way.

Note my reference to a RED light. Two things will send lob-worms back to their homes at the speed of sound—vibrations and direct light from an ordinary torch. But they seem less able to react to red light. With this the worm hunter can work at close quarters, often studying his victims in the full glare of the torch before deciding which end is which of the section above ground.

The basic operation is simple enough. Poise thumb and index finger of the grabbing hand about ½ in. apart. Aim at the point where the worm's body enters the ground, or halfway along the exposed section if you are none too sure. Grab the worm. Hold it for a few seconds. Then, as it acknowledges your superior strength and relaxes, draw it gently from its hole.

If you hunt on lawns lit from buildings and street lamps, you will find the most productive areas in the shadow of parked cars, walls and bushes.

Worms can be kept fit and well for months on end. The simplest method is to fill a box, tea chest or barrel with deep turves. I stress *deep turf*. There must be some inches of soil beneath the grass roots—clay or loam, never sand. The experts, at least, insist that sand and worms will not co-exist for long. Lay the turves lightly, one above the other, to within 12 in. of the top of your box; store it in a cool, frost-free place and moisten the top layer from time to time. Every 12 weeks or so empty the box, replace the oldest turf and toss in a few handfuls of leaf-mould or fallen leaves.

How many worms to a box? That will depend on the box, but it may help you to know that every acre of rich ground is said to hold more than 1,000,000 worms. So who wants a million worms? It's easy enough to be sure of a few dozen, whatever the weather, at any stage of the season.

GHOST FISH

When the hook digs deep into a foreign body one usually knows that it's an old branch or a mass of weed at the end of the line. But as the rod bends, and the current judders against the obstruction moving across its path, there's a fleeting moment of super-optimism. It *might* be a big 'un!

For my part, there is neither surprise nor disappointment as the parcel of weed breaks surface. It was naïve to have expected anything else. Big fish do not behave that way, and I know it, but I guarantee that the next floating snag will prompt the same reaction. It's a different matter when you commence the retrieve convinced that you are into a specimen fish. It happens to all manner of people, and whether the ultimate discovery provokes tears or laughter depends on the individual angler.

Tom Williams tells how he hooked a salmon in fast water—

a really big Avon salmon. He walked it 50 yds. upstream, into safer water, before attempting to play it, and that fish followed like a log—as salmon do at such times—until Tom was ready to get down to business. But this one had no intention of fighting Tom or anyone else. It was an enormous, waterlogged plank!

On another occasion he found one of his fishermen very near screaming point. This poor chap had lost 18 prawns that morning; missed well over a dozen bites. 'Tom,' he said, 'please take my rod. There's a salmon lying to one side of the sluice gate, but I'm dashed if I can get him.' He explained that if the prawn was cast to a certain spot it would swing across to the fish and be accepted in the fast water approaching the sluice. A fresh prawn was mounted and Tom made his first cast. As the salmon responded, he struck, but the line came back empty. Knowing exactly where the fish lay, Tom crossed the river, got the salmon in view and signalled the angler to cast once more.

There was a gentle splash as the tackle hit the surface. The prawn sank in the clear water and moved across-stream, towards the salmon. But the fish never saw it. I doubt if it had seen any one of the lures cast that day. As the prawn moved across the stream it was influenced by the suction of water curling into the sluice and began to move at right angles to its original course. The line would pause, then tighten; and, every time, the current hurled the bait with a resounding thwack against the brick walling. That, of course, was the take. The wretched angler was playing a ghost fish!

I once contacted a fantastic fish in Poole Harbour. If anticipation meant anything, this was the best catch of the holiday. It was a mild, dark night and we were casting well out in the warm-water outfall streaming from the power station. There wasn't a lot doing, but school bass were giving good sport on 6 lb. line and lightweight rods.

At least six times that evening we had tremendous bites, sudden takes that bent the rod in half. Big bass? They might have been, but they were so fast that one had no chance of reacting in time. Just after 2 a.m. I struck at one of these bites and started pumping the fish home. The rod was hard over, the line vibrating with a vigorous 'zz-zz-zer' as I wound in. Out there in the darkness I hadn't the slightest doubt a really good fish was shaking its head to and fro, but still coming in under pressure.

What sort of fish it could be I had no idea, but the excitement was intense and I swear my heartbeats nearly doubled. Seldom have I wanted a specimen as badly as the one I fought that night from the little beach near the outfall. Great sport ... until the lead and baited hook came to rest against a notice board 15 yds. from the shore. In daylight that notice reads 'DO NOT PROCEED BEYOND THIS POINT', or words to that effect. Unseen in the dark, my line had been carried against it by the current, stopped short to give the 'bite', and I'd played it 'zz-zz-zzering' against the pole!

I know one jovial gentleman whose handlebar moustaches are almost part of the landscape on several famous rivers in the South. As a salmon fisher he's first-rate and the moment he has a fish on he lets out a piercing whistle by way of warning to others in the neighbourhood. One bright March day that whistle all-but split my ear-drums. Legering from the opposite bank, I wound in my tackle and sat with Gerry Hughes watching with interest as the fish was played past us, downstream and over the weir. There, in the shallow water, it was brought to a dead stop ... A bicycle tyre in remarkably good condition.

The moral is obvious. Never feel embarrassed if you get snagged or fall for a ghost fish. It happens to us all!

A GOOD THING GOING

If you rule a triangle on the map of Surrey, with Kingston, Epsom and Purley as its extreme points, you are covering ground within reach of thousands of freelance anglers. One of these is Laurie Theobald of Epsom. Laurie has visited many waters over the years, but is fortunate in having a fishery-in-miniature

bang in the middle of that triangle, virtually on his own door-
step.

The lake at Ewell Court is not a large one by any standards,
but is most pleasantly situated and has good parking facilities.
The Court itself is now a baby clinic and public library set in
wooded parkland. If ever a venue demanded strict adherence to
the angling code—with particular reference to the removal of
litter and care of property—this is it.

For roach, carp and tench specialists with only an hour or so
to spare, this bob-a-day ticket water provides an unusual challenge. The Hogsmill river, once famous for its trout, but now
a shadow of its former glory, feeds into one end of this shallow,
clear-water lake. And shallow it is, no more than 3 ft. anywhere
and averaging a mere 30 in. of very clear water. Apart from
space taken by the odd bed of rushes, the bottom can be seen
for many yards from the banks.

Roach in such a water are not to be taken by any hamfisted
angler. They demand fine tackle and the stealth and stillness
of a native hunter. These fish average 12 oz. apiece, with 1½-
pounders in the specimen class. Laurie Theobald admits that
it was only by chance that he discovered how best to catch them.

A few months back he tried laying-on, but a strong wind put
paid to his efforts by blowing his float all over the place. In
desperation he replaced the float with the tiniest of bored bullets,
stopped with a dust shot 'just about visible to the naked eye'.
Line of 2 lb. b.s. and a No. 16 hook-to-nylon completed the rig.
With a pellet of soft cheese on the hook, he cast out and let the
bait settle.

With such ultra-light tackle you do not attempt to tighten up.
Just gather unwanted slack, hold the rod butt ready, place
the top section only in the rest and wait for a tightening of the
line to signal the moment to strike. As it happens, bites were
few and far between with those static baits, which seemed something of a mystery. The bait was clearly visible for the lake bed
is free of weed, and in that still, shallow water the scent of the
cheese must have pervaded the entire swim.

Adjusting his line on one occasion, Laurie accidentally

twitched the bait forward. A sharp knock followed immediately. Coincidence? It might have been just that. He waited, without result and with the line fairly taut, then gave a turn of the reel handle to move the bait yet again. A moment later the line tightened on a really confident bite. Angler and rod responded and within two or three minutes a roach topping 1 lb. was in the net. The time, 11.5 a.m.

Before two o'clock that afternoon Laurie Theobald took 15 roach on a bait that was never stationary for more than 30 seconds. He would cast out, tighten line as much and as gently as possible, then wait. After 30 seconds the reel handle was given a half-turn; a further pause, then another half-turn. Oddly enough, all but one of his fish took the bait as it was twitched for the second time.

This method may produce better than average results for readers fishing similar waters in other parts of the country. It is certainly worth trying in any weed-free swim when established techniques prove unproductive. One can only guess at the reason for success in this case. Why should a slight movement—and it is very slight—cause fish to take so confidently? They were, of course, already in the swim, held there by a light scattering of groundbait introduced at intervals during the morning session.

My theory is that through the summer months these roach have been feeding on aquatic insects moving on the lake bottom. If this is so, any minute movement may be associated with food —a safe, well-tried food at that! They will not hesitate to mouth such 'insects' and move off with them. One wonders how long it will be before Laurie's roach become educated to his tactics. The day will surely come when the line tightens more slowly and shy bites are again a feature on the lake at Ewell Court. Having said that, it may be that the coming of autumn and winter, and the almost complete lack of natural foods behaving in this way, will put a damper on this very effective technique until another summer season is under way.

UNUSUAL—IN BRITAIN!

Carp on fly? ... Carp? They can, of course, be taken on fly-tackle. They *are* taken on fly-tackle in many parts of the world. In my job I have to keep a close eye on comment from overseas. Angling, after all, is international and a news item or a tip from Germany, Japan or America could revolutionise sport for someone in Swansea, Hull or Bexleyheath.

Where fly-fishing for coarse fish is concerned, American anglers lead the way. Not that we really need to go overseas for this brand of know-how. H. T. Sheringham was writing about it before the first world war. Vernon Bates provided a first-class introduction to the subject with his book, *Sporting Tactics for Coarse Fish*, and chub specialists should read Frank Sawyer's first-hand account of chub played on nymphs dressed on ooos!

But let's get back to the carp. There is, for example, a very fine angler in the USA named Mel Ellis. He makes a habit of catching carp of 15 lb.-plus, using a wand of a rod and the daintiest terminal tackle imaginable. I was amazed to read in a recent issue of *Field and Stream* that the nylon leader tied to his fly line is often tapered to a breaking strain of 1 lb.

In the States, millions of dollars are whittled away each year financing efforts to keep wild carp under control. These fish colour great tracts of water as they pig along the bottom, disturbing the mud in their search for food. The mud settles, ruining trout spawning beds. In suspension, it limits light penetration and wipes out acres of food-bearing plants. As more valuable fish stocks decrease so the carp increase, at an alarming rate. It's no surprise that they are taken regularly by trout fishermen and rated, along with the grayling and chub of our own game waters, as piscatorial vermin. But Mr. Ellis had no reason to be concerned with economic considerations. He wanted sport, nothing more, and with standard fly-tackle he found it.

On one August morning alone, he waded the margins of Lake Michigan using dry flies, wet flies and nymphs in turn, to bag more than two hundredweight of carp. He was smashed by many others, but the sport was of such standard that he decided to specialise from then on.

The technique he perfected is similar to that used when nymphing for trout. Rather than flog the water, he hunts for his fish before casting. When river fishing, the nymph is dropped far enough upstream to have it drifting along the bottom as it nears the carp. Timing the strike, it seems, is vital—a knack learned only by trial and error, but which once mastered guarantees the daintiest of sport combined with the maximum of angling thrills.

During the summer and autumn months all species of carp patrol the water in search of food, including floating flies and nymphs engaged in that perilous journey to the surface, where they change into winged insects and take to the air. At times the fish will even nudge stones aside to get at nymphs sheltering beneath them. So the artificial is an obvious lure.

As carp mouth the fly they tend to roll. This seems to be a standard reaction. No less standard is the angler's reply, tightening as he glimpses the flash and whorl below-surface. The result, invariably, is a near miss! Our American friends define the correct drill as (1) keeping a beady eye on the point where fly line and nylon leader meet, and (2) when that section tightens, twitches or skids—strike!

Alexander Wanless, the father of fixed-spool angling, demonstrated that even with the limited materials of pre-war days fly-fishing was possible with light rods and f.s. reels. Shotted line gave sufficient casting weight to sink fly or nymph to the required depth. Float-like controllers gave less efficient sport with the dry fly. With the wonderful range of materials we have available today there is scope for more progress in this field.

It depends on whether you want the fly-fishing of the purist or that of the practical man who must make-do with the tackle he already has. John Bennet of Edinburgh is just such a practical man. A perch fisherman, he fly-fishes with an Arlesey bomb at the end of his line. His lures are made to a special pattern, using trout-fly hooks, red wool and 5-amp fuse wire. The fly is tied in place on a dropper, about 12 in. above the leger weight.

With a nine-foot spinning rod and threadline reel he roams the lochs, gravel pits and canals to the north of our islands to capture magnificent perch. The secret lies not in the fly but the retrieve. Slowly, slowly, slowly ... and the fly wavers in the waters as it follows the line home.

Fly-fishing for coarse fish? As a freelance you can have a lot of fun with your existing fishing gear—and as an introduction to the subject that is probably the best way of setting about it!

WHARVES AND WILLOW TREES

This close season I fished on, and enjoyed it. Different species, of course: different settings and people, but all part of the gigantic jigsaw we call angling.

I travelled miles to sample the tough, night-long sport of eel fishing, with owls hooting in the darkness and rain dripping from the new-green of trees fringing the Grand Union Canal. I followed the same sport much nearer home—around the Docks, in fact—where the mists and night sounds of London's river and the lights and shadows of the old wharves provide a perfect setting for one of Mickey Spillane's thrillers.

On such a night, Dick Murray and I met a man whose home is a magnificent sea-going boat moored in one of the creeks. He, too, is part of our angling memories. Not because of his hospitality and the hot, sweet tea he brought ashore in the early hours, but because he had seen a flying saucer. (Twelve months later I was to have a similar experience while beach fishing at Poole Bay!)

We collected some interesting data along the Thames. At Lots Road Power Station, for example, big roach and eels are often found on the filter screens as water is drawn from the river.

Roach of 1½ lb. are not uncommon there. It would have been enough to know that such fish are sucked in from bankside swims, but the cooling water at Chelsea is drawn through a tunnel leading to the very centre of the river, and the current at that point is as powerful as any a roach angler is ever likely to encounter. But that's where the big fish come from.

Between the eels, conferences and AGMs, I fished for trout like any well-bred angler. I fished in a blizzard at Weir Wood Reservoir and a heat wave at Two Lakes just a fortnight later. And what fishing! With a solitary amber nymph replacing bunched lobworms or deadbait, and with all thought of eels far distant, one lived those moments when the rod lifted into a rainbow trout and pounds of piscatorial dynamite took off on a power run to leap and tail-walk along the surface, glistening in the evening sunshine.

The day after the National Angling Show brought sport that was different again. My fly-only friends may disown me, but facts are facts and there's a slice of the West Country poacher in my make-up. On a tiny tributary of the Upper Thames, flowing through a tunnel of willows, hawthorn and chestnut, I enjoyed trout fishing that has a charm of its own and a worm at the end of the line.

'The stream's thick with trout,' said the bailiff as Jonathan Webb and I prepared our tackle that afternoon. After 40 years on the same water I reckoned the bailiff should know his business. He did. The little river, a foot deep for much of its course and never more than six yards wide, was not without power. It thrust over a bed of pure, clean gravel, digging trenches first on one side then the other as it twisted and turned in that last 300 yards to the Thames.

I set up a wand of a rod—built-cane, as dainty as any brook fly rod—threaded 3 lb. nylon through the rings and pressed on an AA shot. A brandling, lively and very red, completed the ensemble. Roach poles and match rods, shooting heads and heavy coarse-fishing tackle are as useless on this type of water as a howitzer in a two-roomed flat. Wading quietly into the stream I flipped the worm to the top of the nearest hole.

Each yard of water differed from that above and below it. Each ripple had to be studied, fished slowly, as though one had every intention of staying for at least a week. But the first hour produced not a solitary bite. When the break did come it was, of all things, a foul-hooked bleak. Jonathan, fishing 200 yds. below me, fared no better. No matter how quiet the approach, every hole seemed devoid of fish life.

I stood still and silent, the water flowing through my legs, for quite a while. Then at last I spotted a trout lying under a willow clump. So, they really were there! The luck changed and fish came to the net like peas from a pod; wild trout, each weighing 12 oz., give or take a dram.

All evening the swallows zipped under the trees, skirting my rod as one more sapling to be dodged as they hunted the stream. At the close I had four trout in the bag and had returned three more and two chub. Each one of those trout was beautifully spotted, gold-flanked and black backed—the back being an unmistakable characteristic of the true Thames trout. As I said to Jonathan when we met by the car, it seemed a shame that all the fish in that stretch were little fellows, so uniform. At which, modest character that he is, he reached quietly into his satchel and lifted out a one-and-a-half-pounder!

'EASY NOW, EASY!'

Always, I talk my fish to the net. I did it with the first chub I ever caught, at New Bridge on the Stour many years ago, and the habit has persisted ever since. It's, 'Come on, my beauty ... buckets of time ... OK, you go that way ... easy now, easy!'

Goodness knows why some of us carry on these one-sided conversations, but I swear that there's a greater sense of control, of 'feel' for the fish at the end of the line, when I indulge this particular whim.

With any decent fish those few seconds following the strike

PLATE 6 (*top*) Clear-water worming, a skilful and dainty art. A 3½ lb. brown trout taken by the author from the Hampshire Avon—fair game on 3 lb. nylon and a light rod. PLATE 7 Watched by his dogs and a visiting angler, Alex Behrendt of Two Lakes, Romsey, moves a section of the black polythene sheeting (8 yds. × 16 yds.) with which he eliminates weed growth. Agricultural merchants stock these sheets.

PLATE 8 (*top*)   Bill Taylor's little trout rod—5 ft. 10 in. of built-cane weighing only one-and-five-eighths ounces. It is a 'Lee Wulff' of American design, supplied by Farlows Ltd. and by Sharpes of Aberdeen.   PLATE 9   The rod in action on Lord Mountbatten's water: a pool on a River Test carrier stream. Norman Faulkner of New Milton plays a hard-fighting rainbow as the rod's owner crouches with the net.

are moments of tremendous excitement. Perhaps it's the sense of anticipation, the feeling that this particular fish to which the rod bends and the line runs steel-straight in salute, could be the catch of a lifetime. Whatever the reason, alone or in company, I invariably exclaim 'Fish on!' once the hook goes home. Alone, I am wasting my breath. Sharing a boat or with a companion fishing close by, I expect the other chap to do exactly as I would—wind in fast and avoid the risk of crossed lines.

At a recent forum the panel was asked to name the most common fault in coarse angling. My contribution was the thought that many anglers are in too much of a hurry to get their fish to the net. I stand by that. So often one sees a fish hooked successfully, the rod going hard over—all too hard and no music from the reel to compensate—then straightening with a slackening of line that tells its own story. And the conversation between man and fish ends with just two words: 'Oh, no!'

Sometimes, of course, the line holds. The wretched fish is winched in, full of fight and ready to grab any opportunity of breaking free before it is bundled into the net and lifted from the water. Such an angler fails to use his tackle to best advantage, rod or reel. He knows little of the thrills to be had from playing a fish properly, and the tragedy is that he will lose a high proportion of the best fish he ever hooks. I do not suggest that any fish should be played until it's all-but dead. But there is a definite point in time when it can be brought safely to the surface; when it will not thrash like a mad thing or smash the line in a split second of uncontrollable fury as it sees you or the net.

There is a point when you can safely manoeuvre that fish close-in, so that the final act of bringing it over the net and lifting it high is a smooth and satisfying conclusion to a worthwhile encounter. It is difficult to define, but where sport-fishing is concerned I do think that one's ability to feel for a fish culminates in the decision that that moment has arrived. The fight is over. This applies to every freshwater species I know, except the eel. A good eel you will never play out. And this grand finale must be sensed and judged right if the fish is to be landed without risk and yet not too late for its own good.

It's a climax often killed stone dead by those good samaritans who spend their days thumping along the bank netting other people's catches. They seldom ask if you need help: if only they would! The sight of a rod bending is enough to jerk them into action without a second thought for their own tackle or chances. And the first you know of their participation is a series of earth-shaking vibrations as they come panting along the bank, slide down to your swim and aim their net at your fish.

If I was a keen matchman I would insist on one addition to most of the club rules I have ever read: 'That only in extreme cases shall any member net another member's fish and then only when requested to do so.' It might break a practice that is a common feature of club fishing. It would certainly give many more anglers, and young anglers in particular, the chance of playing good fish from start to finish.

'Hold on,' say these helpful Charlies. 'I'll get him.' Many times they do just that, but I'd like a fiver for every fish lost at that stage of the operation—not to mention the shoals of unseen, unhooked specimens which decide that such activity cannot be healthy and beat it for quieter swims.

Under normal circumstances I am not given to talking to myself. But when the 'I'll-net-him' types are around I confess to holding muttered conversations with the rod-butt, reel-seating or float-top; dark thoughts that could never appear in print. Which is a pity. It might persuade some of these slap-happy netsmen to leave well alone. I like netting my own fish!

PART THREE

TACKLE

THOU SHALT NOT COVET ...

There was a time when I fished as light as any angler in Britain, worming and spinning for trout, grayling, perch and chub with rods of seven and eight feet, rods so whispy they react like living things the moment a fish takes bait or lure. My line range was normally 2, 3 and 4 lb. And 4 lb. was heavy. Fly-fishing was never a problem, for the same seven-footer casts a heavy line as far as I want it to go. Fly or fixed-spool, my gear was a joy to handle—until I met Bill Taylor, social secretary of Christchurch Angling Club.

In the summer of 1969 I had a date with Bill and his angling partner, Norman Faulkner. We were to fish a River Test carrier stream stocked with rainbows and wild brown trout. It holds a few grayling as well, but those are on the small side and best forgotten.

The rainbows weigh up to 6½ lb., with a near-record catch that summer of a solitary eight-pounder, and the rules called for dry fly and upstream nymph only. But there wasn't much room for casting. 'Bring a light rod,' said Bill, 'you'll be doing as much tracking as casting on this stretch.' That suited me. My 7 ft. cane rod was hand-built for the express purpose of tossing flies into tree-lined spaces that would put a permanent wave into a reservoir angler's toes. And until Bill Taylor came on the scene I was very proud of that rod.

Fully mindful of the 11th commandment ... Thou shalt not covet thy neighbour's rod, nor his reel, nor any part of his clobber ... I watched Bill take his tackle bag from the car and draw a one-piece rod from its billiard-cue travelling case. Many a light-tackle merchant has written about 'a wand of a rod' when describing things that are telegraph poles by comparison. Bill's is a faery rod, a thing of beauty the like of which I have never

seen before. But I'm bound to add that I took one look at the
water to be fished and didn't go much on his chances of landing
a big one. Even so, I was more envious of that 'miniature' than
I care to admit.

It's a Lee Wulff, supplied by Farlows; a single 5 ft. 10 in.
length of absolutely perfect cane, forming the slimmest,
daintiest weapon imaginable. *It weighs one and five-eighths
ounces.* Can anyone make a rod lighter than that? (See Plate 8.)

A dry fly enthusiast, Bill Taylor set up a No. 6 floating line,
for which the rod is designed, attached a leader tapering to
3 lb. and tied on a Blue Upright. A No. 6 may seem heavy for
such a rod, but as Lee Wulff—one of America's star anglers—has
pointed out on numerous occasions, the line for an ultra-light
rod is usually heavier in proportion than that used with a normal
fly rod. The object is to get enough weight into the air to work
with on relatively short casts, for unless the utmost skill is
employed, long casting can overload and damage these little
rods.

As we walked towards the water Bill offered to loan me his
rod for an hour or two. No angler can make a nicer gesture than
that! I took it from him, felt its slim cork handle, marvelled
at the craftsmanship that had gone into its making ... and
handed it back again.

For most of its length the stream was no more than 12 ft.
wide, often less. It was overhung with bushes, trees and a pro-
lific growth of bankside foliage. Its depth ranged from 6-12 ft.
in the main channel. Halfway up, a pool had formed below a
dam and although we'd seen several wildies it was not until
now that I spotted the first rainbow, a fish of 3-4 lb., looking
as safe as houses under a raft of weed.

We moved upstream without casting to it, taking turns for
a while at fishing the topmost pool, a deep water encased in
trees and bushes that almost blotted out the sky. There was just
one gap where it was possible to cast a short line. I netted a
three-pounder and not wishing to hog Bill's favourite spot, moved
back to the weed raft. The trout was still there, but it was a
devil of a place to fish. The only thing for it was to dig my heels

into the bank some way below him, go into a half-crouch, pray that I would not fall in and cast upstream to the back-eddy in which the weed floated.

The nylon leader landed on the weed pile. I held my breath, gave a slight tug and a sigh of relief as the nymph came clear and was accepted without a second's hesitation. That fish weighed 3¼ lb. As I walked upstream with it I saw Bill's rod bend to the take of a really big trout. Norman Faulkner, who had joined him, beckoned me to hurry.

If ever a fish demonstrated the thrills of ultra-light tackle, that one did so. It ran out of the pool and downstream for at least 15 yds., with Bill applying side strain via the natural springiness of the rod. Not for a moment did he let the line pull directly against the reel or allow the rod to bend at too acute an angle. His fish came back; it made for the far side; dived to the bottom, then took off on a Wall of Death circuit round the pool. I got the landing net ready, but the fish wasn't, yet. Norman looked pale and I must confess I felt it. And for all my respect for Bill's angling ability, not until he had played his fish out and brought it finally to the bank did I realise that the fingers of my left hand had been crossed for him—crossed so hard against the net handle that it hurt to get them apart. What a fish! Four and a half pounds of gleaming, multi-coloured rainbow trout.

'Like a blessed salmon,' said Norman.

The little rod was stood on one side as Bill removed the fly. You're a beauty, I thought, come what may I've got to have just such a rod. Norman lit a cigarette and puffed a cloud of smoke into the evening sunshine. 'That must have been a thrill and a half,' he said to Bill. And in a way I have come to recognise as being distinctly his own, Bill Taylor beamed at us both. 'I cannot understand,' he said, 'why more people don't fish with this kind of gear.'

Neither can I.

SUMMER WEED?

For many years the start of the coarse fishing season has been marked by at least one article explaining ways and means of beating the weed. 1967 was no different, but the solution was.

For the man who favours leger tackle, blanket weed presents serious problems. Crust will float above these green carpets, so will chunks of marshmallow—which is fine and dandy if you are satisfied with those baits. If not, you face the prospect of using lengths of polythene tubing, ball-pen refills, foam rubber off-cuts and similar devices. One alternative is the slider float, used all too rarely in these circumstances. And there is another way out, one I can vouch for, having devised and tested it thoroughly through the summer of 1966.

A chance remark by an angling friend produced this unusual solution. At the time, our efforts on the club's gravel pit were being thwarted by a layer of weed that made it impossible to present worm baits to advantage, yet worm baits were essential. At one point I held a specimen lobworm aloft, a king-size helping of first-class fish food ... 'If we could make this float we'd get somewhere!' Loud laughter from the next swim. 'How would you do it, John—stick a straw up its porstomium?' True, that was not his exact reply, but it's near enough to convey his meaning. And the meaning set me thinking.

A straw, after all, is a semi-rigid tube full of air. And what is a worm if not a tube of sorts? It takes in soil at one end and pumps it out at the other. I admit that by Nature's own design a straw is meant to be full of air and light enough to float. What a lobworm was full of, other than partially digested soil, I had no idea, but I was well aware that even an empty one sinks in no uncertain manner.

For the rest of that trip my mind was not wholly concerned

with pit fishing. I kept asking myself what would happen IF a big lob could be persuaded to absorb a quantity of fresh air. Was it feasible? Could a walloping great lobworm be made buoyant?

There seemed to be only one way of finding out. A few days later I acquired a hypodermic syringe and a supply of fresh baits. Persuasion did not enter into it. Firmly held in a piece of cloth to minimise their wriggling, those worms had no option but to co-operate. In went the needle; three or four segments filled with air and—they floated!

I've used this method on all manner of occasions, very successfully indeed. The secret is to avoid injecting too much air at a time; to handle the worm carefully, and to use the finest needle obtainable.

If there's a layer of weed on the bottom, say one inch deep, stop the leger lead 6-8 in. from the hook. The worm will then float and wriggle several inches above the offending greenstuff. If you want your bait one or two feet off the bottom, adjust the line-stop accordingly.

When fish are feeding at the surface the floating lob technique is next door to dry fly fishing. A small worm is recommended, hooked once only at the tail end. With a single 'jab', inflate three or four segments in the middle of your bait and cast out on a light line. Pump in too much air and you will end up with a very dead worm indeed. The evening rise is obviously ideal for this manoeuvre, but it is not always possible to watch that floating bait as the light fades. Fish then with the rod tip held high, the nylon outlined against the sky, and as the line runs tight a firm but controlled strike is enough to make contact.

For the roving angler fishing the warm days of mid-summer, floating lobs have much to commend them. When fish rise to the fly and other insects drifting on the water, a surface lob twitched slowly back to the rod tip can be quite devastating. At other times an Arlesey bomb can be dragged along the bottom— a few inches at a time—with a worm floating 12-18 in. above it. This is one way of presenting this particular bait at the right level to attract many species.

Fresh brandlings and other small worms are too fragile for the Injection Stakes. They collapse too easily and the air bubbles out of them. Wastage is high before one can be found that is tough enough to inject properly. Lobs, fresh or scoured, will float on the surface or as high above the weed as your line-stop permits, for a considerable period. And by this I mean hours at a time. No tubes or foam rubber, no Christmas trees at the business end of one's tackle. Just bait-up in the usual way, reach into your little black bag, and start fishing.

FLASH AND FLUORESCENCE

I once suggested that in Britain spinning is not as popular as it might be, due to the shortage of open waters. Not even the most anti-social angler would try to spin the pegged banks surrounding many of our larger towns and cities. Frankly, I am no longer sure that this is the only reason.

Colin Willock, who has produced more quotable quotes than any other angling journalist I know, once wrote: 'Float fishing is essentially passive; spinning is downright aggressive.' As I recall his theme, float fishing is more akin to trapping than hunting, the angler waiting patiently for fish to find and take his bait. The spinner, on the other hand, quarters the water, searching every hole and every bankside swim until he makes contact. Perhaps Colin was right. Perhaps spinning does not appeal to the majority of Englishmen simply because they *are* passive in their reactions to just about everything.

And yet, where spinning is concerned there is still so much to be learned, in spite of rods, reels and other tackle that make accurate casting relatively simple. Looking at some of the catalogues recently issued, I wonder if the range of lures isn't too extensive—way ahead of our knowledge and skill in this branch of angling. What do we know, for example, about the use of different colours and designs? What do we know about light and its effect on various metals and the fish we hunt?

One man who devoted years to such research was 'Seangler' —Hampshire's John Garrad—who between the wars developed a specialised technique for flounder fishing. His book, *Sea Angling With The Baited Spoon*, will repay study whether you spin for flounders, bass, perch or pike. Few anglers have ever presented such detailed and worthwhile records. At one stage John Garrad experimented with spoons of four different materials. He noted consistently that towards nightfall they ceased to be effective in the following order: copper, brass, plated (chromed), and white-painted spoons.

'In other words,' he wrote, 'copper ceased to attract fish almost as soon as the light began to lessen; brass took fish a little later. Plated took well into the dusk, but the white took fish almost up till dark.' How many of us ever stop to think of these things, let alone carry white-painted spoons in readiness for the final stages of the day's sport?

Fishing under a bright sun, John Garrad found that flashing, plated spoons caught no fish at all, but one of tarnished brass got results. In more brilliant light a red-painted spoon succeeded even when his old faithful of dulled brass failed totally. In this he confirmed the advice of salmon fishers. For nearly a century these chaps have smoked the surface of their spoons to a dull, non-reflective sheen when fishing in ultra-bright conditions.

I was reminded of these theories recently as I waited to be served at Gerry's Tackle Shop in Wimbledon. Two young anglers were selecting a few Droppens, the ABU lure that is really a brass Arlesey bomb with a treble mounted below the weight and a spinning vane or attractor revolving above it. These spinners are ideally shaped, of copper, silver-metal or black, and the larger of those two boys knew which to buy, or thought he did. He took one from his friend's hand and put it back in the rack. 'Black's no good,' he said. 'You gotta have flash to 'tract fish.' In fact, you gotta have a fair variety to cope with the subtle changes of light and underwater conditions.

Efgeeco have a marvellous Scandinavian spoon with an unpronounceable name, but an unmistakable pattern. It's 3 in. long, of orthodox oval shape, with a dull silver or gold hue on the inside surface. But the outer surface is finished as an imitation perch, and for big perch and pike this spoon is productive in a wide range of lights.

Exactly the same considerations apply to plugs, including floaters. But what rules hold good for plastic worms, plugs, hooks and shrimps made of fluorescent materials I cannot say. On occasions they may scare the living daylights out of every fish in sight. I'm equally certain that many times each season these weirdies will beat orthodox lures on every cast.

The conclusion to be drawn from all this is a very simple one. Before tying on that Mepps, Droppen, Toby or a trusty spoon of your own design, look up. Note the light in the sky; the light reflected from the water. Does it call for a bright silver lure, one of medium tone or something with no flash at all? That one decision could be the making of a good day's sport.

PEBBLE-SHAPED LEGER WEIGHTS

Leger fashions come and go. The swingtip has almost put paid to the finer art of touch legering, and the now popular link leger must have slashed the sales figures for Arlesey bombs. But there's one method yet to be fully exploited. The buoyant leger. Call it a slow-sinking or wooden leger; call it a balsa bomb if you like fancy labels. The end-product is the same— a combination of wood and metal counterbalanced to take the bait slowly to the bed of a stillwater fishery and rest lightly on the bottom. It's a technique that often catches fish when heavy-leger tactics fail, for the slightest movement lifts the buoyant leger with minimum resistance to a fish making off with one's tackle.

Capt. L. A. Parker of the Hampshire Avon—'Skipper' to a thousand anglers who fished Downton before and after the

1939-45 war—did a lot of experimenting with slow-sinking legers. I'm not suggesting that Skip Parker invented the buoyant leger. He didn't. But in *This Fishing*, published by Cleaver-Hulme Press in 1948 and again in 1960, he defined the basic theory as well as anyone has ever done.

Parker made the point that when fish are 'mad on' you could leger with a flat iron and still catch them. As most of us know only too well, fish are usually more cautious, even super-cautious. And that's when we need the feel of a tight line. 'Try to visualise the state of the bottom in most stillwaters,' he wrote. 'It is either mud, silt or weed, or a combination of two of them. Imagine how detrimental a lead can be when a fish makes off with your bait—often held only between its lips. You get a bite all right, but how many do you miss? It's not to be wondered at if lead and line are embedded on the bottom. No matter how slight the obstruction, drag is bound to occur as the fish moves. And this is one of the main difficulties when long casts have to be made.'

And since you must have weight for those long casts, Capt. Parker went on to illustrate his slow-sinking leger; a piece of soft wood, 3/4 in. long by 1/2 in., drilled through the centre to take the line and fixed at both ends with lead shot to give a complete counterbalance. In the intervening years there have been many variations on the theme, but none as neat as the one I received from Roy Christie of Wimbledon.

Roy's pattern is shaped like a flat pebble. Carved from mahogany, it has an overall length of 2 1/2 in., a maximum depth of 1 1/4 in., and is about 1/2 in. thick at its widest and most central point. A brass tube of 1/8 in. diameter runs through the centre. 'A strip of lead—enough to make it sink very, very slowly—has been inset across one end of the pebble. The object in placing that inset weight at one end is to create a planing action on the retrieve. The slightest pull is enough to lift weight and hook clear of weed, silt or other forms of obstruction. The finished version has been painted and varnished to give as professional a design as one could wish for. There's a market for this piece of tackle: manufacturers please note!

I cannot imagine anything better for deep-water reservoirs, especially when perch are well out from the banks and may be shoaling at almost any depth available to them. No self-respecting fish would refuse a worm presented in this manner—that mahogany pebble flutters to the bottom as slowly as a freeline bait. Readers wishing to copy Roy Christie's design should note that the weighted end is placed nearest the hook. Roy paints a bright yellow dot—shown in Fig. 4—to give immediate identification, and the pebble is stopped on the reel line with a small lead shot fore and aft.

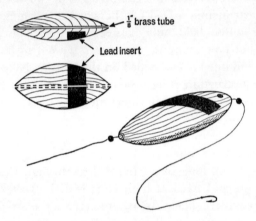

FIG. 4   *Pebble-shaped leger—Roy Christie's design*

A freeline bait or one weighted by a single shot providing a fixed leger in miniature, should suffice when fish are feeding close-in. But for distance casting in lake or reservoir, and even harbours at the stand of the tide, this slow-sinker is well worth using. It may seem a contradiction in terms, but fishing with a heavy weight on his line Roy Christie has got as near to long-distance freelining as any angler is ever likely to get. His design is neater, easier to handle and a lot more efficient than the separate leads and soft-wood legers of earlier prototypes.

DEATH BY THE YARD

We are in trouble. It seems that a campaign is being mounted against the practice of discarding unwanted hooks and nylon. I would like to report that this campaign is the work of the National Anglers' Council, the National Federation of Anglers and other representative bodies. Alas, no! The impetus comes from authorities outside the sport—the Lord Chamberlain's office, the RSPCA and various local councils.

The People, one of Britain's big-circulation Sunday newspapers, has joined the fray. I do not agree with all the views expressed by their columnist, 'Man o' the People', whose trenchant pen has fought many admirable campaigns. But I concede that such comment is necessary. Nylon is the deadliest litter in the world. We all know that birds can so easily tangle, beyond hope of ever gaining their freedom, with the almost invisible strands hanging from bush and tree. We know, too, that a discarded length of nylon can snare and maim all manner of creatures, wild and domestic. For many of them, a slow and agonising death is inevitable.

Sea anglers are also involved, here and in America. More and more cases are being noted of boats breaking down, their propellers fouled by coils of monofilament. A recent news item quotes the story of two skin divers who risked their lives to retrieve the body of a companion from the wreck of the *Oregon*, 10 miles off the New York coast. There was no way of establishing the exact cause of death, but that rubber-clad body was cocooned in nylon strands.

Each and every one of us faces an obligation we have known about and endeavoured to meet long before *The People* and others came on the scene. Every angling newspaper has stressed the matter over and over again. Thousands who read the angling

Press have instructed young enthusiasts, warned fellow members and recorded the facts in club newsletters. This we must never stop doing.

Ron Minion, acting secretary of the National Federation of Anglers, is quoted by *The People* as saying, 'All our members are taught to clear their lines from hedgerows and trees.' He then defines the guilty parties with that oft'-repeated, hoary old stand-by ... 'They are not regular anglers.' Nonsense, Mr. Minion, nonsense! I've fished waters—and so, I suggest, have you—that could only be frequented by regular anglers. Again and again I have found and destroyed odd lengths of this death-dealing synthetic. But I share and acknowledge Ron Minion's opinion of carelessness that can produce such horrifying results. It's a simple matter to coil unwanted line around one's fingers; to snip it into short, harmless sections. Better still, put the hank of line into a 'screw' of newspaper and burn the lot. But don't throw it away.

For the sake of our sport and its prestige at this time, let's have no more references to anglers who aren't really anglers at all. Every Association and Federation, every angling club in this country, can contribute far more by launching a determined anti-litter campaign among its own members. Bottles, cartons and waste paper are bad enough, but all anglers, whatever their interest in the sport, must recognise one basic fact ... WHERE WILDLIFE IS CONCERNED, NYLON IS THE DEADLIEST LITTER IN THE WORLD!

HOOKS GALORE

When I go fishing, the rod I use may cost anything from a fiver to fifteen pounds. The hook tied at the end of my line is worth, at most, a few coppers, but if this all-important item retailed at five or six shillings we would all pay a lot more attention to it. We'd expect to have each hook checked under a magnifying glass before parting with a penny. Fortunately for us, reputable manufacturers are more than a little jealous of their good name; the products and the service they offer are both first-class. Mustads alone deal in more than 65,000 hook patterns, so if your dealer cannot supply what you want, ask around—the perfect hook is there somewhere!

John Goddard of Efgeeco tells me that in past years his Company has met with strong opposition—from anglers—to the introduction of weedless hooks and spinners. I find this incredible, but JG is not given to joking about such matters. The prime objection is that hook guards—usually two stand-off wires protecting the hook-point—are likely to deter fish from taking the lure and may even prevent a clean bite.

This is nonsense, of course. A powerful predator, attacking a flashing, wobbling spoon, is not going to be put off by two delicate lengths of steel wire runing parallel with the hook shank, nor will it feel them on the take. I doubt if it would even see them: the average treble is far more obvious in the water. If you are fond of spinning, give guarded hooks a thorough test. There are several excellent patterns on the market and I guarantee that you'll snag at least 50 per cent less often *and* catch more fish. Make no mistake, one follows the other.

The water you cover with these lures is going to be less subject to disturbance and the lure itself will be in action, actually fishing, for a proportionately longer period of time. Another point, and it's a bad one for the Trade, is that you'll spend less money on spinners and spoons. Good hook guards are very springy and as they brush against the majority of underwater snags they bounce the spoon up and away, clearing the obstruction. An unguarded hook, single or treble, will bite deep into the floating branch, weed mass or whatever type of snag your fishery may specialise in.

In the past few years I've had numerous inquiries from anglers seeking barbless hooks. Mustad make them in sizes 1 to 22. The extreme sizes may present difficulties, but mid-range hooks can be ordered from and supplied by your local dealer. If 'Barbless size 8' is not good enough for him, the following catalogue detail should leave him speechless ... 'forged straight, turned down tapered eye, bronzed, extra fine wire without barb'. And when you fish, keep a tight line or take the consequences.

With many hooks, a barbless state can be achieved by 'crunching' the barb between long-nosed pliers. The resultant bulge on the bend helps to keep the fish on, but makes disgorging a very simple matter indeed.

Even where hooks are concerned there are absurd differences between one river authority and another. Why these people cannot agree a basic set of rules, applicable to the entire country and fully cognisant of the times we live in, is beyond me. But this they seem unable to do. Each authority is its own master and those who fish these tribal territories must be aware or beware. Check local regulations, for some include strict rulings as to the size of hook that may be used, especially for salmon, trout and eels. Many areas have no such regulations: but then, it must be said that many areas have no fishery management either!

PRESS CUTTINGS ARE WORTH KEEPING

We met just above the bridge, both seeking trout along the middle reaches of the Hampshire Avon. A friendly greeting was followed by the offer of a drink and some moments later I learned that this chap's first love was match angling.

'I keep a mass of Press cuttings,' he told me. 'Mostly details of venues, different swims and conditions at various times of the year and, of course, tackle and tactics that have paid off for other matchmen. The problem is finding enough time to paste them into my scrapbooks. You must use cuttings, John: how do you manage?'

Many matchmen keep a small library of newspaper cuttings yielding information that is often of tremendous value to them.

Now I'm no match angler, but for once I felt that I could contribute something of value. My casual acquaintance was right about the journalist's need for 'clips'. How else can one give a precise quote three years after the speaker opened his mouth or put pen to paper?

Scrapbooks I do not recommend. They take too much time—pasting-in and indexing—and if a complex subject is being investigated you need nine fingers on each hand to separate the pages and refer quickly from one cutting to another. It's far better to keep loose cuttings and devote an individual file to each subject. One may be marked Tackle, another Groundbait, others Match Venues, NFA Knockout Competition, and so on. But when you want information on a particular item all your cuttings are together and can be sifted through in quick time.

Mark each clipping with the date and the name of the paper from which it was taken—'*Angler's Mail*, 8.5.70'. Most Press stories will include the word that appears on your file cover; for example, 'Billy Lane's groundbait on this occasion was a mixture of currants and primrose petals ...' If Groundbait is the subject just ring that word in pencil. In this way, when you have to consider a mixed bag of cuttings, taken from various files, they can easily be sorted afterwards and returned to their correct holders.

File covers are expensive: I never use them. Take a single page from any tabloid newspaper and fold this almost in half. Punch two staples along each side and there's a file cover, free of charge. Note that I fold the page *almost* in half. In fact, I overlap one end by nearly an inch since this makes it easier to open the file and also provides a suitable place on which to write-in the subject concerned. Stand your file covers in a box or cupboard and keep them in alphabetical order. Nothing could be simpler. For a few minutes work each week—literally minutes—and with no outlay of any kind, other than the cost of your staples, you'll have a most efficient reference library.

Angling today involves a steady traffic in tackle and ideas right across the globe. That's no bad thing; there's a lot to be said for knowing how sportsmen in other countries cope with problems common to us all. For example, an American fly-fisher named Larry Green faced a situation most of us have encountered at one time or another. After several days with limit bags the trout were as scarce as spinning tackle at an All-England Championship—for no apparent reason.

Hard fishing eventually produced one or two small rainbows, each stuffed to the gills with caddis larvae, complete with the tube-like homes these creatures camouflage with grit, stones and tiny pieces of vegetation. A major hatch of caddis fly was under way and the trout were pre-occupied with this food-form to the exclusion of all others, including Larry Green's artificials! As the caddis emerged to begin their journey to the surface so the fish were waiting for them down on the bed of the river.

There are apparently 2,500 different species of caddis or sedge-fly in the USA. The British list for these moth-like insects is nearer 200, but the same pre-occupation must occur in our waters and at such times Larry Green's tactics could save many a blank day.

He went back to the water's edge, collected a handful of empty caddis cases from among the gravel and sat up most of the night tying flies equal to the occasion. Using No. 6 long shank hooks, he mounted the natural caddis cases and carefully packed each one with cotton wool soaked in waterproof glue. Invariably, it proved necessary to put a slight bend in the hook shank before it would fit the case properly. Three or four turns of glossy black hackles below the eye of the hook imitated the legs of the emerging insect. The tying silk was then wound many times and lacquered to resemble the grub's shiny head.

Next morning there was no shortage of trout. This most unusual fly—half-natural, half man-made—was a real fish-getter. The purists will no doubt wish to imitate the caddis larva with feathers and tinsel. Indeed, there may already be such dressings. Those less lily-white may think as I do, that an inch of fine tubing can be camouflaged very effectively with materials that Nature would choose. It might even occur to some blackhearted bounders in our ranks that if the cotton wool packing is replaced with fine lead wire the lure would be heavy enough to cast and play along the bottom from a fixed-spool outfit.

If caddis might be so treated why not corixa, amber nymphs, polystickles, wormflies and various other dressings in their season? Every one could be self-weighted to the equivalent of a swan shot if need be, without appearing too grotesque. The inclusion of a hook guard in the dressing, giving a weedless lure, is not beyond our ingenuity. With a fixed-spool, light rod and nylon line, a swan shot can be cast a country mile.

Why not attractors tied to Butcher, Teal Blue and Silver, Peter Ross and other dressings weighted just sufficiently for sporting fixed-spool operation? Skilled angling for game fish need not be the prerogative of heavy-line fishermen. The idea has much to commend it, adding to an armoury that already features floating plugs in great variety and still more plugs and spinners for mid-water use. By comparison, these weighted flies and lures would be relatively tiny. Their use will depend for the most part on accurate casting, coupled with a life-like retrieve between weed banks, through deep holes and—with caddis-and-case— along the bottom.

The old-type bubble float was discredited by the purists as little more than an excuse for long trotting with wet or dry flies. In all truth, that is not the whole of the story, but in general terms I think they were right. The degree of skill involved was very slight and the wake those floats set up made it virtually impossible to play the fly on the retrieve. Self-weighted flies are a different matter. They suggest a technique yet to be fully explored and requiring considerable skill; a technique for which the roving angler's fixed-spool outfit is admirably suited whether

he hunts the aristocratic trout or the gamer members of the
coarse fish family.

JUST A PIECE OF WIRE

If you are short-sighted or your grip is none too sure, threading
a line through the rod rings may be no easy matter at the best
of times. In a high wind it can be sheer murder!

It is surprising how many anglers take the end of the line
between thumb and forefinger and pass it through as though
each ring was the eye of a needle. Short-sighted or not, you will
find it easier and quicker to loop the line back on itself, grip
the two strands and feed a short loop through the rings.
Naturally, it's so much stiffer than a single piece of nylon.

True, the top ring on many a rod will not take a loop, but at
that stage the job is almost done and the straight single-end can
be threaded through. The only difficulty is when you let go of
the loose end, once it's through the rings, while you sort out
floats, hooks or leger leads.

Overcoming all these problems is a gadget sent to me by Mr.
C. P. Evans, ex-licensee of the Hope and Anchor Inn at Mans-
field, now resident at Scarborough. It's a time- and temper-saver
if ever there was one; worthy of a place in any tackle box. Perhaps 'gadget' is the wrong word. Mr. Evans's line needle is in
every sense a tool-in-miniature. It is capable of many variations,
but let me first describe it in the terms of his original pattern.

A piece of stiff, steel wire, just over three inches long, is the
raw material. One end is filed to a sharp point, the other is
hammered flat and then folded back on itself and tapped down
until only a tiny gap remains—just enough to grip the line
tightly. That's all there is to it. With this, threading nylon
is the simplest of operations even when your fingers are frozen
to the marrow.

The alternatives are obvious. A piece of green twig, cut from a nearby tree or bush, will do the job. A single, slanting cut, two thirds of the way along its length, serves to grip the line as your 'needle' goes through the rod rings. At a push, a piece of coarse grass would do, but a sliver of hard cane or plastic would be a more permanent choice.

For all the alternatives, the sharp-pointed needle-like pattern of the original Evans design is undoubtedly the best. Once the line is in place that point can be pushed into the edge of your tackle basket, the ground, under a reel seating or even (may the saints and all purists forgive me!) into a cork on the rod handle. It holds the line captive while you, with both hands free, sort out the terminal tackle in your own good time.

SPIN-LEGER . . .

Spinning with artificial lures was not introduced as a sport until the middle of the last century. The baited spoon technique, favoured by many who spin for flounders and other sea fish, is of still more recent vintage, although I'd hazard a guess that our forebears used it way back in time. At some unrecorded stage in our development, an early member of the angling fraternity may have dislodged a shell lined with mother-of-pearl; watched with interest as it sank in the water, and noted the speed with which predatory fish moved to attack. Whenever and wherever this happened, Man at that moment registered the reaction of fish to brilliant, moving objects. And since that day anglers have experimented with variations on the original theme.

There was, for example, the late Capt. L. A. Parker—'Skip' Parker of the Hampshire Avon. Years before the First World War he recognised the value of flash and brilliance, not in the form of spinners but as eye-catching fragments mixed with groundbait. Skip Parker's research was very thorough. At every opportunity he used his water telescope to study the habits of fish in their natural environment. He noted that anything white on the bottom attracted them more readily than other colours. 'I could see them come out of their course,' he wrote, 'to look over the white object.'

On the Thames and in the clear waters of the Avon, Len Parker developed his theory into a practical, match-winning technique. His fish-stopping whiteness was obtained by stamping on a sackful of oven-dried eggshells, quantities of which were an essential ingredient of his groundbait mix. 'Eggshell,' he wrote, 'sinks readily and remains put, lodging between the pebbles. Every piece to the fish looks, perhaps, like something to eat. If it only attracts one fish on the off days, that one may open its mouth to your bait.' So, with spinners and groundbait particles we find brilliance acting as an attractor. It is not unknown for a bare hook to be fished through the water like ... what? A solitary smallfry?

But spinning involves more than flash. Movement and vibration must be considered. Perch and pike will mouth bread and other unlikely baits as they are wound in, but ignore them while they lie on the bottom. I've had legered maggots, lobs and chunks of crumb taken in this way, as no doubt you have. By contrast, whatever else an Arlesey bomb or a string of swanshot may do, they do not glint or flash, nor are they designed to wobble enticingly on the retrieve. Nothing moves less naturally than a leger lead! But if we could make that lead an attractor, results may at times be far more encouraging.

Which brings us back to the flash and brilliance of the baited spoon and to Skip Parker's groundbait mixture gleaming on the bed of the river. Why not combine the two? Having only recently started experimenting with this method I can only outline the theory involved, but I do suggest that it may be worth trying at many venues. It should certainly prove worth while where roach or bream share the water with jack or large perch.

Briefly, the leger weight is replaced with a spoon from which the treble hook has been removed. The spoon is mounted on a swivel through which the reel line is threaded and stopped in the usual way. A single hook is tied direct to the line and the bait hangs below the spoon on a short trail.

As a leger weight, this rig operates in the same way as any other—except that a passing fish could indeed be attracted by the glint of the polished spoon resting on the bed. That fish may be a roach, bream or perch. It swims close in, realises that the reflected light comes from a harmless, non-edible object, and then spots the bait. If our fish accepts, the reel line will run freely through the swivel, just as it would with a link leger or any other kind of leger weight. It is on the retrieve that the spin-leger comes into its own, for it then functions as a baited spoon, the blade flashing through the water with the hook close enough to be engulfed by any predator with a notion to attack.

With this type of rig the leger man who aims to search a wide area of water gets the best of both worlds. He fishes with maximum advantage even when retrieving his bait. Give it a thought. For that matter, give it a trial. You can spin through an arc of water then rest for 10 or 20 minutes while the legered bait does its work on the bottom. All this without making a single adjustment to your terminal tackle!

WORTH THE EXTRA

Waders and a three-quarter length PVC coat, with a muffled scarf and a sou'wester, provide a wind-cheating, rain stopping outfit that allows more freedom than I could ever enjoy beneath a king-size umbrella. But then, I'm not a regular match angler. I can rove at will, and do! But this is not an article on the different approaches to the sport. I want to discuss something far less controversial ... footwear.

Match angler or freelance, nothing could be more vital to personal comfort and well-being, yet it's a subject seldom mentioned in the angling Press. I admit the choice is limited. You can have waders or gumboots, and on the face of it there's precious little to be said about either of them. But as one who invariably wears thigh waders in the winter months—even on a towpath!—I'm constantly amazed by friends who comment on them and talk of 'getting a pair one day'.

Mine are quite ordinary rubber-soled Streamfisher's—well-lined and less bulky than those with studded soles. They suit my kind of fishing, and if I have to travel by public transport they can be rolled up and packed, without too much weight, into a canvas grip. On the other hand, if you intend clambering about on weir aprons or wading streams bedded with boulders and large stones, my choice is not for you. Solid, hobnailed soles will give you better service and save many a slip.

Why this preference for waders? Apart from the occasional need to take to the water in search of trout or when trotting down at some venues, two factors make them a 'must' for winter fishing. They're warmer, much warmer; they're rainproof, especially around the knees. Having said that, let me advise strongly against unlined waders. Condensation is a serious problem with the unlined variety and they are the coldest things this side of Siberia. Being formed of a single layer of rubber they tend to be so flimsy that pin-prick punctures appear like spots in adolescence.

A duck-killing, trout fishin' friend of mine claims that he has yet to find a wader that will last more than a couple of seasons. This has not been my experience. Good waders repay reasonable care. I'm an idle character by nature, but I make a point of washing my boots the moment I return home. They are then stood in a corner, soles uppermost, on a pair of broomsticks, and after two seasons of really hard wear my latest pair is 'as new'.

As to punctures, I have fished rough country along the Kennet, the Avon and one or two estuaries without sustaining so much as a pin-sized hole. Gravel pits are the worst spots, with exposed flints, old metal and timber ever ready to establish contact. No doubt I shall become aware of a leak one day. The answer is to visit the nearest tyre depot and have the puncture covered with a vulcanised patch. My colleague, Gerry Hughes, once owned the most-patched pair of waders in Britain, but they had served him well through 10 seasons of intensive fishing and somewhat rugged treatment.

If a new pair is more than you can afford, keep an eye on the local auctions. There are bargains to be had. Some months ago a friend of mine bought a magnificent pair for 12s.—his first and final bid since no one else had the slightest interest in them. They had one leak which cost 5s. to put right. Brand new, the same pair would have carried a price tag in the region of £7.

Whether you use gumboots or waders there are times when woollen socks are too warm for comfort. Even in winter they are inclined to irritate my skin. Try Bootsox. They're really soft slippers, scientifically designed, and they do all the makers claim for them. The problem one faces with any kind of rubber footwear is that perspiration condenses on the inside of the boots, moistens the socks—no matter how thick—and slowly chills the feet. With Bootsox the perspiration passes as vapour through layers of non-absorbent nylon and polyfoam, on through an outer layer of cotton material to condense on the inside of the boot in the usual way. As moisture forms it is absorbed by the Bootsox's outer covering of cotton or wool, but held from one's feet by the polyfoam barrier. Nothing could be simpler or more effective. With waders one's feet and ankles can be warm and comfortable wearing only thin nylon socks— the Bootsox taking the hard wear inside the foot. Incidentally, they wash well and should last two or three seasons.

A final point for those who have yet to go in 'over the top'. Put spare socks in a nylon bag and push them to the bottom of your rod holdall, now! That way they can never be left at home. One day, drying off after a ducking, you may be glad you took the trouble.

CUT YOUR OWN WEIGHTS

There must be 101 situations in which a baited hook, with no weight whatever, could be used to advantage—if only one could get the darned thing through the air and into the water at the right spot. It might be a deep channel, far out in a gravel pit. The trouble with this kind of water is that the fish, perch especially, may be at any level down to 40 ft. or more. Weight is needed to get the bait into position, but once it hits the surface that weight is the angler's undoing. It carries the bait downwards at an unnatural speed, and even if perch were attracted by its entry into their domain they would not necessarily pursue it to the depths at which it finally settles.

In theory the solution is easily defined. We need a weight that will allow us to cast in the usual way; it must then part company with the line and leave the baited hook to sink slowly and naturally. Lumps of clay, pressed into place around the line? Too chancy. All too often the clay sets off in one direction, the bait in another. And what guarantee have you that the clayball will break up?

Given the right wind and current, there's fun to be had making 'boats' out of slices of bread, dock leaves, water lily leaves or odd pieces of timber. These will carry the bait across the water until the line is tightened, the rod point lifted and one's terminal tackle persuaded to abandon ship. The little ship technique does work, but the angler is at the mercy of wind and current. Like the clay ball idea, it is not sufficiently precise for regular, pre-planned attacks on these difficult spots.

SALT is the answer—lumps of common salt. The method I use is by no means new, but it's one many readers will not have encountered before. I will not attempt to lay down hard and fast sizes: these vary with the distance to be covered, and the tackle and bait used. If the aim is to cast a light bait—a single maggot perhaps—30 yds. without lead or float, this is one way of doing it. A block of household salt costs between 8d. and 1s. From this you can cut at least 20 casting weights, more when fishing at close quarters where the problem is not weight-for-distance but just enough to swing the bait into a precise spot. True, at such times lobworms provide their own weight and plenty of it. But not everyone wants to use lobs.

The one essential in preparing a block of salt is a knife with a serrated edge. This will cut the raw material as smoothly as you could wish. A bread board makes an ideal base. Saw and cut the salt block into five slices, then divide each slice into four. Scrape the corners of each piece to give a streamlined finish and carefully—very carefully—bore a hole through the centre with a meat skewer. Pack your casting weights in a damp-proof container. This is important, but even more so, see to it that they are carried in a tin or box that will give some protection in transit. Rock salt is firmer than you might think, but it will not withstand too much buffeting about.

Simple to prepare, the weights are just as easy to use at the water. Set up your tackle for free-line angling. Then fold the line to give a half-loop a few inches above the hook. Push this loop through the hole in the salt weight—a disgorger is useful at this stage—and as it comes out at the other end slide a matchstick into place to prevent the folded line from pulling back again. Held in this way the weight will stand up to the most energetic casting. As it hits the water so the salt absorbs moisture and quickly disintegrates; the matchstick floats clear and the baited hook sinks slowly to the bottom.

In a river or stream the current will carry the bait as it sinks under overhanging branches, floating weed or flotsam. In a deep pit there may be no current at all: once the salt has broken up the bait is free of any resistance to a taking fish. Line movement signals bites very clearly, and since a run can be expected at any time don't be in too much of a hurry to rest the rod or yourself!

THE FLEET'S IN!

What with Frank Guttfield's tin-can flotilla and Gerry Savage with bait-rafts fashioned from polystyrene tiles; Jack Hilton's dear little sailing boats and Kenny Ewington's miniature Kon-

Tiki rafts, we shall soon need a mate's ticket before applying for a rod licence. Now, I see, Bob Church has joined the boarding party, with thoughts on using balloons to get his baits into distant swims.

All these techniques are sound enough on occasions. I thought that everyone had at some time or another floated a bait into inaccessible swims, using a chunk of breadcrust, a piece of stick or bark as a makeshift boat. It's often the only way to get a spinner among tree-shaded chub along the Hampshire Avon. But reaction from readers shows that these unorthodox tactics do not meet with universal approval. They are, I suspect, a bit too off-beat for some people. But not all. Guttfield, RN, had no idea of what he was starting!

In February, 1969, Features Editor Gerry Hughes asked what I would say to the story of an angler who had spent £130 building a radio-controlled boat for the sole purpose of shipping herring and par-boiled potato into deep water. 'It sounds an expensive hobby,' I replied. 'Are you sure someone isn't pulling your leg?' Gerry read the letter again and pronounced it genuine.

That Sunday, with every stillwater within miles frozen solid, I drove under Vauxhall Railway Bridge, took the fourth turning on the left and, finally, knocked on the door of Sidney Bond's flat. To be honest, I was none too sure of what to expect. A wild-eyed genius with a yen for mechanical angling? A mad scientist with visions of a 150 lb. pike in the depths of some remote Scottish loch? Sid Bond, 55-year-old head bailiff and vice-president of Addlestone Angling Society, didn't fit that picture at all. And the neat little flat shared by Sid and his wife—and their stepson, carp specialist Fred Thorncroft—bore no resemblance to the trailing wires, soldering irons and workbench paraphernalia I was convinced lay beyond their front door.

We talked fishing at some length while I thawed the ice from my bones. Then Sid left the room, to return a few moments later with 'ELECTRA : LONDON' suspended from a canvas carrying frame. I'm no model-boat fan, but I could so easily enthuse over this craft. Four feet long and perfect in every detail, on stillwater she answers to 12-channel radio control at distances up to a mile from base. Fitted with port and starboard lights, Electra is powered by two 6v accumulators coupled to provide a maximum of 12v. This gives absolute control, forward or reverse, and no noise other than a low-pitched hum as she glides across the water.

When I saw the boat she had a three-sided metal tray mounted aft, the open end of the tray facing the stern. It was large enough to take a whole herring and snap tackle. A bait placed in that tray could be carried, say, 80 yards out with the bail arm of Sid's reel open, then gently pulled clear as Electra reached the fishing grounds. I asked if line stretch created problems at that distance. Sid reached for Jim Gibbinson's latest book, *Carp*, thumbed through the pages and came up with the information that ten per cent line stretch could indeed be expected.

Reaching across the sofa I adjusted the tiny fenders protecting the moulded fibreglass hull. It all seemed a far cry from tin cans and ceiling tiles. But there was more to come.

'I'm thinking,' said Sid, 'of fitting a maggot spreader in place of the tray. It would allow us to groundbait a wide area far out from the bank. She'll carry float or leger tackle, of course, and that pulls free easily enough.' I looked at Fred Thorncroft. A keen angler, member of the National Carp Club and of Zaandem Angling Club, near Amsterdam, Fred has travelled far in search of big carp. 'It's beyond me,' he said. I must admit, that was how I felt.

The owner of such a craft needs a GPO transmitting licence —£1 for five years—before going into action. And if he intends operating outside a fixed five-mile radius the Post Office requires at least fourteen days' notice. The correspondence between a roving angler and the Postmaster-General would be good enough for *Punch*. 'Dear Mr. Stonehouse. As I shall be fishing the Norfolk Broads in two weeks' time . . .'

There seemed nothing that this boat could not do. Her motors looked like the inside of a minature computer. 'It is a minature computer,' said her proud owner. 'So,' I asked, 'what happens when she breaks down 50 yards out?'

I should have known better. Such things don't happen to a craft as 007-ish as this one. If the power supply falls below two-thirds of the amount needed for normal operation a special circuit comes into play. This takes over from the remote control unit standing beside Sid's rod rests and ferries the boat to the nearest landfall, ready for a change of batteries. It was a remarkable piece of engineering. Sid Bond, Cap'n Guttfield, Gerry Savage, Jack Hilton, Ken Ewington and Bob Church should get together sometime, in convoy. We might have an annual match for mini-boat anglers.

Beautiful and superbly-built though she is, and perhaps a pointer to the fishing tactics of Tomorrow, I could not fit Electra's trim lines into my idea of a good day's fishing. But that's angling: all things to all men. Answering to remote control, the spotlight on the cabin roof played across the table. 'Now stop talking, Dear,' said Mrs. Bond, 'and let Mr. Piper enjoy his tea.' I did enjoy it. But we were still talking two hours later!

ONE TO BEAT THE TIP?

It takes time for a new angling technique to become established. The swing-tip is an example. Produced by Jack Clayton some years ago, the tip was used only by a minority of leger men until quite recently. Successes in the All-England did much to boost its popularity. The main objection voiced by the anti-tippers—that it hampers smooth and accurate casting—is seldom heard these days and whatever relegates this indicator to second place will have to be very good indeed.

In all this I am not discounting the dough bobbin and variations on it. There is a multiplicity of designs—corks armed with hair clips, pingpong balls weighted with lead shot, and plastic baubles in glorious two-tone colouring. In one form or another

PLATE 10 (*top*) World Champion in 1963, Billy Lane of Coventry within a dram or two of realising a long-standing ambition. Four of these specimen roach topped 1 lb. 15 oz., but stopped short of the 2 lb. mark. Part of his best-ever match fishing bag of 46½ lb. caught during a match on the Hampshire Avon between the Longford Estate syndicate, *Angler's Mail*, Downton Anglers and a team from the Avon and Dorset River Authority.
PLATE 11 Dave Swallow's answer to *Tie Me a Fly!* The proprietor of Custom Tackle, Bournemouth, specialises in saltwater and pike-fishing flies of superb quality. His Swallow Squid is action-packed; even the eyes move!

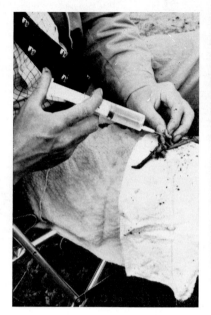

PLATE 12 (*left*) How to make a lobworm float. Air injected into three or four segments gives a surface lure that will wriggle for hours and is of particular value to carp, chub and perch anglers at certain times of the year.
PLATE 13 (*right*) Mullet on spinners. In some waters a baited hook assures maximum returns. A size 'o' lure is best but these fish will attack surprisingly large spinners. Mullet and sea trout in Christchurch harbour found even this model and its size 6 treble not too large.

PLATE 14 Afloat on Poole harbour in the wind-blown spray of a December day. Whether on salt or freshwater, there's a lot to be said for messing about in—and fishing from—boats!

the bobbin remains a firm favourite. If ever Man fishes on some distant planet you may be sure that the bobbin will feature in his tackle, even there. But today the swing-tip holds pride of place in more sophisticated angling circles and only one indicator has the least chance of jolting its supremacy—the Spring.

Around Manchester and Leicester, and along the Thames valley, the advantages of Don Hill's invention are becoming evident. Introduced in 1966, the Spring is the simplest of warning systems. It functions quite separately from the rod and line, and consists of just 15 in. of sprung wire shaped to form a half-circle. At one end is a clip or alternatively a screw-fitting for attachment to any standard bank stick. At the other end— the free end, so to speak—the wire is bent to form a distinct 'V'. Line rested across the half-circle of wire slides down until it rests in that 'V', where it holds the sprung wire under tension. A bite, tugging at the line, makes the wire dip sharply.

In the past I have often dispensed with the dough bobbin and laid my line across a conveniently placed reed or twig at the water's edge, bites being signalled as the reed dipped downwards. The Spring works on exactly the same principle. It can be fished in all conditions suitable for swing tipping and reacts perfectly when the tip could be used only with difficulty.

Every leger man knows the problems of adjusting a bite indicator against strong-flowing currents. True, the swing-tip can be weighted and will still give an adequate signal more often than not, but not always. Bobbins can be made heavier, but getting the weight just right takes time, trial and error, and once the strike has been made the whole process may have to start all over again.

With the Spring no such problems arise. *Strike: replace line: carry on fishing.* The line drops easily and quickly across the wire, ready for the next bite. Fast-water adjustments are entirely automatic, the wire being tensioned by pressure of water against the line. It is the only indicator able to set itself by natural tension and still leave enough movement to warn that the bait is being sampled.

Many tackle ideas look good on paper, but flop when put to the test. Not this one. Don Hill and members of Eclipse Angling Society developed the prototypes under battle conditions, fishing with them to the point that rival clubs talked of Eclipse going 'leger mad'. Mad or not, they took some fabulous bags and won many a match with the new technique.

While developing their skill with this new tool these boys also knocked hell out of post-war theories about the ideal length for a leger rod. Using the Spring with a short bank stick one must sit well back from the water or fish sideways on. That's no hardship, but the long bank-sticks developed by Eclipse —jutting out over the water—have overcome this problem. So have the five- and six-foot rods they use with a normal bank stick. Say what you will, results belie those who insist that no rod under ten feet is worth considering. As a bite indicator the Spring deserves far greater popularity.

RAISE YOUR GLASS . . .

Several years ago, every self-respecting angler was expected to record air and water temperatures, and the experts of the day wrote magazine articles suggesting a link between the mercury's reaction and the golden key to successful angling. At one point the enthusiasts established that fish would not feed at temperatures below a certain level, but the joy was short lived. Some 'ornery cuss set out to fish water at least four degrees colder and landed a bag of chub that made all the statistics look silly.

The extent to which light penetrates the water was also considered. Photographic light-meters were commonplace and much valuable research was carried out by anglers and scientists alike. I thought then and I still think that this factor has great bearing on our sport, for it governs the movement of plankton, the growth and reaction of oxygen-producing plants and the visibility of our baits. But of one thing I now feel certain: temperature and light are not the key factors.

This search for a universal measurement by which to record, compare and forecast conditions influencing the sport intrigues many anglers. I fancy that the answer is linked with something we've known about for years—barometric pressure. In Britain we have one of the most variable climates in the world, so much so that at one water the sun will shine all day while storms make fishing a misery only forty miles away. The sport at the two venues will be very different: so will the barometer readings. Situations of this kind are typical and they spring from small areas of high and low pressure moving across the country in an ever-changing pattern.

All wild creatures react to variations in the weather, fish more than most. I remember three days of glorious copybook fishing a couple of seasons ago in which a friend and I had big bags of roach and perch. On the fourth day, in apparently identical conditions, we got nothing. When I returned home that evening the glass had gone back a fraction and late that night the weather broke with a vengeance. I hadn't sensed the change many hours before, but the fish had. They'd gone off feed and moved to safer, deeper water. It may be that at such times there is little point in tackling-up until the barometer starts to rise once more.

No doubt you have sensed the sudden stillness as a storm approaches. Duck and wildfowl can be heard, but with few exceptions the songbirds are silent. As rain threatens you raise your brolly and cover your tackle bag; the float rides at anchor as if stuck fast in a sea of glue. A scattering of raindrops ring the surface, then down it comes! But after a while you *feel* the pressure lift; the air is suddenly fresher, cooler, and as the skies brighten you cannot help but notice that the birds are singing their heads off. And when songbirds are active, fish will feed.

There is a close link between the reactions of fish and bird-life. Apart from any question of storms, I have noticed repeatedly that on days when birdsong is subdued and few birds fly, sport is often, but not always, sub-standard. The reverse is seldom true, and if the birds are active as I approach the water I reckon to hum a melody myself—there's good fishing ahead.

One other point prompts the thought that anglers have instinctively known the value of barometric pressure for a very long time. Consider these times . . . (a) 4 a.m. to 10 a.m.; (b) 10 a.m. to 4 p.m.; (c) 4 p.m. to 10 p.m.; (d) 10 p.m. to 4 a.m. I suggest that if you had to select any two of these periods as being ideal fishing times you would plump for (a) and (c) without much hesitation. Of course you would—they cover the morning and evening feed.

I am assured that even when a static front exists throughout a 24-hour period, a sensitive barometer will still react at different stages of the day. The glass will, in fact, rise during the periods we associate with the best conditions (a) and (c) and fall during those when angling normally produces least results. So the barometer as a scientific measuring instrument confirms what we and the fish have always known to be true.

There remains the $64,000 question—to what extent does that confirmation indicate this instrument's research value at times of uncertain and rapidly changing conditions?

QUICK-CHANGE LEGERING

One of many readers' letters to reach me in recent years contained a novel solution to an age-old problem—a leger rig allowing a quick change of weights with the minimum of fuss and expenditure. It's a variation on the link leger devised by Bert Ravening of South Oxhey, Hertfordshire.

Bert is such a complete handyman that with the exception of hooks he seldom buys anything readymade. No swan shots or Arlesey bombs in this man's tackle. He works with small sections of lead-covered electric cable, usually 3/16 in. to ¼ in. in diameter, removing the wire core and snipping the outer covering into tubes of different lengths and weights. But first, let's consider his nylon link. Two loops are tied in, one at each end, and one of these loops plays a vital part in the quickest quick-change technique imaginable.

Each of the tubular leads has a small flap cut into one end with a pair of scissors. The nylon link is threaded through the tube, the flap raised and one of the loops in the nylon slipped over it. The loop is then pulled tight against the base of the flap and held in place by pressing the lead back into position.

To change weights one has only to lift the flap, remove the loop and slide another lead into place—the whole operation taking rather less time than is needed to read this sentence. It is, I think, a completely original approach to the question of leger tackle and terminal rigs. With it Bert Ravening has taken chub, bream and roach in plenty on private waters at Rickmansworth and on many stretches of the Thames. A keen member of the Carpenders Park Angling Club, he won the Marlow Rose Bowl competition in 1965-66, fishing, as always, by legering with a dainty 7 ft. 6 in. steel rod—the 'Ross' by Accles and Pollock—and varying his weights according to the current. His catches include a 15 lb. carp, some very big bream and a 12 lb. pike, yet he never uses anything stronger than 4 lb. line and his tackle is always home made.

Even the sliding ring that holds the link on the reel line is home made, cut from 3/16 in. polythene tubing. Each ring is about ⅛ in. wide and is fastened by the remaining loop in the nylon link. Before fixing the lead the nylon link is threaded through this ring; one loop is pulled through the other and the nylon tugged tight to hold the ring in place. This tubing cost about 4d. a foot from any big ironmongers. Four pennies: the total outlay for ninety-six rings!

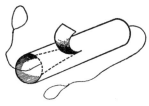

FIG. 5 *Quick-change leger*

As for line stops, a ¼ in. strip of polythene, cut from the same tubing, is notched on either side and attached to the reel line by a simple clove hitch.

When I first saw these tiny, elongated leads, they looked like a miniature version of the 'long leads' used in the fast-flowing rivers of Italy. Those Continental leads range from 6 to 18 inches in length, sometimes more, and hold bottom far better than any rounded leger weight. Bert confirmed that in flood conditions he has used 1 oz. leads of this type with great success when orthodox leger weights proved useless. His theory is that the water flows *through* his leads, turning them lengthwise in the current and so reducing resistance to the main flow.

It must be said that Continental anglers seldom bother to strip the wires from inside the lead covering. Their great leger weights are plain chucks of electric cable attached by a nylon loop of lower breaking strain than the reel line. With Bert Ravening's idea it would be a simple matter to use an extra-long link and thread on two, three or more of his hollow leads, according to the current, fixing the last one in place with the lead flap.

MEASURE THE DEPTH IN ONE

I once asked who invented the Lift method of float fishing. Letters poured into the offices of *Angler's Mail*. They referred us to books, magazine articles and local know-how going back a century or more. Then came a letter from Mr. L. James of Walthamstow, London, pointing out that the Old Master himself, Izaak Walton, described the basic technique in his chapter on bream fishing. Walton didn't call it the Lift, and he measured his silk and horse hair lines in rod lengths, but there it was—the quill submerged except for a half-inch tip and the lead firmly on the bottom—back in 1653.

For all that I know, the three-ring floats sent to me by Mr. A. H. Slade of Plumstead, London, are based on theory and practice every bit as ancient. Be that as it may, I have never heard of them before, nor have I seen such floats offered for sale. These three-ringers function most effectively as slider floats, operating against a line stop in the usual way. Some might question their sensitivity compared with single-ring sliders, but Alf Slade catches fish in plenty.

The float's main purpose is to provide an accurate and speedy method of plumbing the depth in one simple operation. This it does, outdating the plumb lead and tied float. There's no need for several casts before a correct setting is obtained, and water disturbance is kept at a minimum. One cast is enough. If necessary *that* could be made from behind cover without even seeing the water!

Alf Slade uses this pattern in his search for carp and tench in Dartford Lakes. Sea fishing, too. I gave the samples he sent me a thorough testing in swims of known depth, both near the bank and far out: they worked perfectly. My sketch shows the three rings positioned in such a way that the float will slide on a slack line. When the line is pulled tight it 'locks' the rings. The float cannot move, up or down.

A fairly heavy weight is tied to the end of the line after threading the nylon through the rings, top ring first. A large Arlesey bomb is ideal for freshwater, but take care that it's matched by the strength of your rod top. A small shot, nipped in place a few inches above the weight, will prevent the float from fouling lead, swivel or knot. To find the depth, the tackle is swung gently into the swim and the reel line slackened off. As the weight hits bottom the float starts its climb to the surface and settles there within seconds. All that remains is for the angler to gather slack line, tighten firmly to the weight on the bed of the swim, and reel in, keeping the line absolutely taut. The float's position marks the exact depth—all you have to do is decide where to place your line stop and tie it in without further delay.

FIG. 6
Alf Slade's
three-ring
slider float

Alf Slade makes his own floats, and very neat they are (Fig. 6). In fact, any straight quill or balsa float can be adapted, using no more than a length of fine wire, whipping and varnish. The secret is to avoid making the diameter of any ring larger than ⅛ in., and to ensure that both top and bottom rings are set as close to the float as possible. Whipping is easier, and the finished job is a lot neater, if the straight ends of the wire forming the rings are tapped flat— to lie flush against the side of the float—before tying them in position. Incidentally, the stand-off ring in the middle should protrude at least half an inch from the side of the float.

I was interested in this idea as a means of plumbing distant swims on my home pit. For reservoir specialists also, Alf Slade's method should prove of the utmost value. One day's fishing was enough to convince me of its worth and I have no doubt that many readers will second that opinion.

Its use is not confined to individual anglers intent on a day's sport. Consider the number of clubs fishing gravel pits and deepwater lakes whose members haven't the foggiest idea of the precise depth of any given point. Isn't this float the answer to at least one close season task? All that is needed is a large-scale map of the water. The working party can then be split into pairs, each pair being allocated a section of bank and equipped with Slade-pattern floats, lead weights, a notebook and a pencil. In one pleasant and interesting day every stretch within reach of the banks can be charted to the inch.

What happens when the depth of water exceeds the length of the rod? You wind in until the float hits the rod top, gather the line into your left hand and draw it tight to the handle. Then slacken line by making a reverse half-turn with the reel, at which the float will slide down and rest against your left hand. Tighten-up again and wind it back to the rod tip before repeating the operation. Do this three times with a 10 ft. rod and the water in front of you must be 30 ft. deep!

TEST CURVE BALLYHOO

There's been so much nonsense written about the test curve theory, it is not surprising that some anglers are completely baffled. In fact, there's not a lot to it. Those who treat the subject as some advanced form of piscatorial mystique are kidologists of the highest order.

As a first step, let's establish the reason for bothering with test curves at all. Their purpose is simple enough. Ideally, there should be a state of balance—an inter-relationship—between the rod, line and the weight cast. The test curve is the key to a simple formula which defines the limit of each part of our tackle and protects the most important item of all, the rod.

An experienced angler can pick up a rod, get the feel of it and decide what line strength to use. At the same time he can state the approximate weight he would be prepared to cast with that rod. In practical terms he wouldn't be far out and the chances are that the exact test curve would confirm his views. Since good rods are expensive, confirmation is worth having.

The newcomer may be less confident. He doesn't need me to tell him that if he casts a 4 oz. lead with a slender-tipped built-cane rod either the line or the rod top will be damaged, perhaps both. And if he hits into a big fish, using line of 2 lb. b.s. on a carp rod, that line is going to snap long before the full power of the rod can be brought into play. Conversely, if he hooks the same fish on 10 lb. line, using a rod designed to carry only 4 lb. nylon, the line may hold but the rod will take a hiding from which it may never recover. Balance is vital. Only when we know the test curve figure can we start talking of balanced tackle in the more familiar terms of line strength and casting weights.

There is no secret about the position in which the test curve is decided. You start with the rod firmly held in the hori-

zontal position. Weights are suspended from the tip and added
to, a little at a time, until the rod bends and the top section
is in line with the vertical. *The amount of weight required to
bend the rod into that position is the test curve figure measured
in pounds or ounces.*

Let's assume that it takes 16 ounces to make our rod tip point
straight down the line. We can now say that the rod has a
one pound test curve. But the fact is meaningless unless trans-
lated into practical terms, that's easy enough. *Casting weight:*
For every 1 lb. of the test curve weighting we can expect to
cast up to 1 oz. of terminal tackle—but no more. For continuous
casting two-thirds of that weight is normally recommended,
and to exceed this is to risk permanent damage to the rod.
Line strength: Multiply the test curve weight by five. The
resultant figure indicates the ideal line strength for that rod.
With a 1 lb. test curve the answer is, of course, a 5 lb. line. In
fact, you have some leeway where line strength is concerned.
There is a difference between dry and wet strength, and lines
are subject to wear and tear. As a general guide we can work
to a difference of one-third between the dry strength and that
applying while actually fishing. So, a rod with a 1 lb. test curve
will react happily to lines ranging from 7 lb. to 5 lb. Anything
much above or below those figures must be out of balance.

For the average angler there is no need to go farther. I
remember listening to a fierce argument at the last National
Angling Show about the shape of curve produced by tip-action
rods as opposed to those with a through action. Believe me,
where everyday fishing is concerned such things are of no
consequence. What matters is the weight needed to achieve
that curve.

Some makers note the test curve loading on their rods. It's
an idea that should be universally adopted, for how else can
the customer know the maximum casting weight and the ideal
line for the rod he is being asked to buy?

I believe the theory of test curves originated with French
rod makers during the inter-war years. Back in the 1930s Hardy
Bros. Ltd. linked with Alexander Wanless, giving a similar rating

to the rods he designed at that time, but their test curves were arrived at by a slightly different procedure. All these figures can be made to sound like very advanced scientific data. In fact, they provide a simple method of ensuring that one's tackle is well-balanced and the rod free of excessive strain that would otherwise shorten its life.

POSSIBILITIES AFLOAT

I have a yen to own a boat. Not a big one; not one of those gleaming, streamlined beauties powered by twin 200 h.p. outboards. Not, that is, unless I inherit a small fortune. Like many anglers and all yachtsmen. I know exactly what Water Rat, of *The Wind in the Willows* fame, had in mind when he said, 'There is nothing—absolutely nothing—half so much worth doing as simply messing about in boats.' But Water Rat didn't go far enough. Messing about in boats is fun: fishing from your own small craft is real-life adventure.

It's an ambition not without snags. For the city angler even a 7 ft. dinghy presents storage problems. It cannot stay on top of the car indefinitely and would, in any case, be too small for my purpose. As a flat-dweller, with no garage or private garden, I'd find it easier to house a pet alligator. But I still want that boat.

It is true that a dinghy can be kept at permanent moorings, leaving one to find space at home for nothing more than the oars, outboard motor, life jackets, first aid kit, compass, distress flares, charts, reserve petrol can, plugs, spanners and all the bits and bobs essential to the safety of the boat, the owner and his passengers. In any case, for the roving angler permanent moorings are not ideal. From the moment you tie-up for the first time you are saddled with that particular stretch of water.

The boat can, of course, be moved from one venue to another, either on the roof of one's car or by trailer, but the weekend's

fishing is short enough without making a slow run to the home
harbour and an even slower run to distant waters with the boat
in tow. My interests are largely freshwater—coarse and fly—
with a growing fondness for the estuaries and creeks along the
South and East coasts. These vast tracts of water offer high-
quality sport yet to be appreciated by thousands who could so
easily fish them during the summer and autumn months.

For estuary fishing to be enjoyed to the full a boat is almost
essential. And when it comes to buying one, personal considerations are as varied as the patterns in a tailor's shop. My basic
requirements demand a craft that is relatively inexpensive,
easy to store and move about, capable of carrying one passenger
with complete safety and suitable for use on rivers, lakes and
estuary waters. I have not the least intention of heading out
into the Channel under my own steam.

Let me enlarge on that point about freshwater venues. Many
excellent fishing spots are beyond the reach of bank-bound
anglers. A small boat, powered by a carefully handled outboard
motor—5½ h.p. would be my choice—is the passport to these
quiet places and many pleasant days' fishing. Who knows,
catches at such spots may even be above average—and the way
some of our rivers are fishing lately, they need to be!

Don't assume that because you can move freely up-river you
have the right to fish every yard of the way. On most waterways the fishing rights are the property of those owning banks
on either side. Anchor your boat, start fishing without per-
mission, and you run the risk of being charged with poaching.
But for the angler afloat the roving game takes on a new con-
cept. To wander a mile or two of bank in the course of a day's
sport is surely the limit for a fisherman on foot. By contrast,
the small-boat owner can try his luck at widely separated points.

There's a lot to be said in favour of a lightweight two-man
craft, and judging by a fistful of brochures and a great variety of
Press articles my final choice will involve one of the top-quality
inflatables. The Commandos were using a much larger version
of these boats when I was last in Poole Harbour. Like theirs,
the small craft are sturdy enough—with the proviso that one

must keep a weather eye open and not venture too far afield. Inflatables have obvious advantages for the city angler. They pack into a valise. They can be stored in a cupboard or out-house. They fit the boot of one's car and blowing them up is no problem—a special valve can be fitted to one of the plug sockets in the car engine. Switch on, and air pumps into the dinghy.

It does seem that there's no such thing as the perfect craft. Select how you will, you cannot have everything. But for readers facing domestic problems similar to my own these tough, super-buoyant inflatables have much to recommend them.

PART FOUR

MANAGEMENT

FIRST-AID FOR FISH

Somewhere in Middlesex there's a pike that owes its life to a man whose childhood ambition was to be a surgeon. Charles Franklin never realised that ambition, but he came pretty close to it. War service with No. 40 Commando was followed by years of study and a Doctorate in Pharmacology. From time to time, his research work into the liver—human and otherwise —includes surgical operations on animals, which brings us back to that lucky old pike.

Assisted, as always, by Alec Viner of Silver Wings AC, Dr. Franklin and his mobile laboratory were engaged in a routine survey of a club water. Investigations of this kind call for analysis of the water, nettings to provide evidence of existing fish populations and their numbers, checks on disease and parasites, scale readings and measurements to determine age/growth data. The club must provide its own labour, be it six men or sixty, and those with experience of handling fish— the scalesman at club matches, for example—and members with special knowledge of the fishery, receive priority. Fish taken from the nets for detailed examination are kept in galvanised tubs prior to being measured, weighed and returned to the water after scales have been removed for later study under the microscope.

On this occasion Charles was busy at the table when a pike of about 10 lb. was placed in the weighing basket. The fish promptly leapt into the air. As it fell back, it caught the side of its jaw on the edge of the wire tray. 'A 10 lb. pike is no fairy,' said Dr. Franklin. 'This one fell in such a way that its own weight ripped its jaw open. In fact, the lower jaw was hanging off.'

Club members were dismayed. But for the accident here was

a fish that any one of them would have been proud to capture; a fish in prime condition, and a good one for that water. Several of them urged Charles Franklin to 'kill it: put it out of its agony'.

As he told me later, he had little doubt that those watching were more distressed than the fish, and since this was a stock fish of some value he took the view that if it could be saved, it should be.

Pike do not show the tenacity of other large fish when removed from their natural habitat. Carp and tench can be kept out of water for surprisingly long periods. And they travel better than pike. If this fish was to remain an asset to the club, something had to be done quickly. Charles soaked a large towel in water and swathed the pike in it, wrapped from tail to gill casings, with only its head showing. 'That towel,' he said, 'was enough to keep the fish alive and well for about half an hour.'

With a suture needle, thread and surgical forceps, he put four-teen stitches in the pike's jaw. He literally sewed it together again. The wound was cleansed and treated with an antiseptic—Acriflavine—and the fish released. To the delight of those who watched the operation, the pike recovered and swam into deeper water, moving strongly and apparently none the worse for the experience. As the survey continued—this one lasted several weeks—all concerned kept a close watch for that particular fish to reappear in the nets. Worse still, they feared that one day they'd find it floating belly-up or dead on the bottom. In fact, it was not seen again and is assumed to be in the water to this day. No doubt Old Scarface will eventually fall for a plug or deadbait and the fact will be entered, with regret, in the club records.

Would such an operation have an adverse effect on the fish? I think not. Its forward 'radar'—that network of sensitive pores visible on a pike's jaw and forming part of the lateral line nerve system—may not function as efficiently as before, but for practical purposes all systems would be as near Go as any pike could wish. Wrapping the fish in a wet towel, and keeping it wet, played a vital part in reducing shock, excessive movement and dehydration of body tissue.

The incident was recorded on cine film and was probably unique in the annals of fishery management. As Dr. Franklin stressed to me, this was no gimmick. Any competent angler could have done the same thing with forceps, needle and thread, and a desire to avoid killing a fine specimen. To put a fish 'out of its agony' is a normal and well-intended reaction. As this story shows, it's not always the best course to follow!

HOW TO WRECK A GOOD FISHERY!

Harvey Torbett is a man of parts: author, biologist, war-time commander of a minesweeper, film director, schoolteacher and an angler of exceptional ability. Not least important, his sense of humour is way above average. All of which adds up to a character who is usually the life and soul of a fishing party. But as we gathered in the bar of the Woolsack at Hunton, Kent, Harvey was deep in thought. He beckoned me to one side.

The theory he outlined is one I have not encountered before. It concerns a problem faced by many clubs: stunted fish. For months past Harvey had pondered every aspect of this matter. He is convinced that in many cases where heavily-fished waters become overstocked with sub-standard fish one important factor is too often ignored—groundbait. He considers cloudbaits a particular curse.

Did he think that groundbaiting should be banned at these venues? 'That,' said Harvey, 'is the 64-thousand-dollar question. I do it myself, but I have to say—YES. Within a few years many fisheries would improve beyond all expectations.'

He went on to explain that for nine months of the year groundbait pours into bankside swims, providing millions of minute particles having little or no food value for adult fish.

For the small fry, facing their first hazardous year of life, those food particles represent survival in waters where the natural supply could not possibly maintain them in such numbers.

Without this artificial feeding thousands of tiny fish must perish. Forced to roam in search of natural food, they would normally run the gauntlet of predatory control. Pike, perch and eels, even adults of their own kind, are an obvious danger. Water birds are another. Certain insects kill and devour them. Only a small minority are left to become the pride of the fishery and enjoy their rightful share of available food supplies. But on so many waters the growth and safety of these myriads of fry is assured. They have only to scavenge among the carpet of cloudbait laid by anglers every weekend and replenished on many evenings during the summer months.

Consider for a moment that a handful of fine rusk will keep 50 first-year fish alive for a long time. Before it goes bad still more will be provided. Those midgets survive and develop until a more natural *but less plentiful* diet becomes essential. By then the damage has been done—these are too many mouths to feed. Life is maintained by inadequate foodstocks, augmented by maggots, worms, bread and other groundbaits, but because of the numbers involved growth slows and finally ceases long before it should do. Within a few years the original stock of good quality fish dies off, to be replaced by stunted specimens infinitely more numerous and breeding at a disastrous rate.

To my mind this is sound theory. That first year of life is vital to the culling of fish stocks. Regardless of species, losses at this stage must involve a high proportion of all fish hatched. It may well be true that the techniques we employ in our quest for sport actually eliminate the natural process of selection.

I do not accept that the banning of groundbait is the complete answer, nor do I think that Harvey Torbett had this in mind. It would be a step in the right direction on many pits, lakes and similar waters. But it could be no more than a first move towards sensible management and a gradual transition to top-quality fisheries. That quality can be achieved only if the ban is followed by a sound development programme.

Netting prior to the breeding season will ensure an immediate reduction in numbers and a marked increase in the amount of food available. The introduction of suitable plant life would provide shelter in which freshwater shrimps, plankton, molluscs and insects can thrive. There is no single remedy, but these two points alone indicate that much can be done, and done quickly, to bring about an improvement.

It's quite a thought that on a particular day the use of groundbait may increase your catch. It may even win you a trophy. In the long run it could wreck the fishery!

WANTED! 1,000 NEW FISHERIES

When I was a boy AD 2000 seemed a distant milestone in the annals of science fiction. Now its thirty-two years away and those years are likely to be the most crucial in the history of angling. Between now and then the world's population may double. Estimated at 3,000-million in 1967, by the close of the century there will be so many people that if every drop of rain is collected, stored and put to good use, there will be just enough to meet everyday needs and no more.

Experts declare that mankind faces a major catastrophe. The use of seawater—desalination—is now a practical proposition, but its development requires still further research and capital on a vast scale. For most authorities, cost and convenience are key factors; why bother with desalination while there remains one drop of water to be abstracted from our rivers?

Abstraction will increase as the population does likewise. The social significance of our waterways will seem of less importance as the need to exploit them becomes more urgent. And as Suburbia spreads its tentacles the risk of pollution, deliberate and accidental, will also increase. Already there is talk at high level of 'dispensing' with poplar and willow trees because of the volume of water they absorb. There is talk of covering the larger lakes and reservoirs with a monomolecular film, sprayed on to the surface to prevent loss by evaporation.

Who can doubt that in the face of this treatment many once-popular fisheries will disappear? The toll exacted by natural forces—winterkill, for example—will be slight compared with the demands of a teeming, water-hungry population. Land is not plentiful in these days, but the shortage of water for recreation, for domestic and industrial use, is even more acute. You can bulldoze housing estates and replace one- and two-storey dwellings with buildings reaching to the sky. Water needs a hole in the ground, and worthwhile quantities cover many acres. This is one reason why our efforts to prevent back-filling of gravel pits are proving so successful. But let's not kid ourselves that fishing is the only consideration involved.

In the past, organised angling was slow to react to foreseeable change. With only thirty years to go, and the writing already on the wall, it's time to start talking about small, specialised fisheries. For that matter, it's time to start doing something!

Believe me, there is plenty to be done. All over the country nature is at work turning neglected ponds and lakes into marsh, scrub and then solid ground. Many of those sites could be transformed into magnificent fisheries. Elsewhere, ground unsuitable for building projects can provide splendid angling centres. The Sports Council has cash available for such projects. Earth-moving equipment can be contract-hired for less than you may think. And contrary to popular belief, you do not need resident biologists, chemists and water engineers—or the financial resources of a regional association—to tackle the job.

Expert guidance may be had from several organisations, some government-sponsored, some private. The end-product calls for a mixture of know-how, commonsense and sheer hard work, plus determination to turn a wasteland into a place of value and beauty. The Americans are today more conscious of this situation than any other nation on earth. In their country massive programmes are under way to improve existing fisheries;

to build and stock new ones, at a speed that leaves us standing.

But one does not have to look overseas for the proof of the pudding. *Angler's Mail* published the story of Southgate and District AS, a North London club who set out to find a derelict lake and make it their private fishery.

One of the highlights of the Club's history was the question posed by a member battling through the undergrowth in search of water.

'Where is this bloody lake?'

Answer, from the man with the map: 'You're standing in it!'

In two years these enthusiasts from Friern Barnet converted a tree-grown swamp, its banks shattered, its two-and-a-half acres hidden under scrub and bramble, into a venue most clubs would have been proud to own. Their capital resources were slight, their membership less than fifty, and when it came to doing the job the labour force varied between a dedicated half-dozen and a maximum turn-out of twenty men. But they succeeded.

Two Lakes, the now-famous Hampshire trout fishery, is another example. There, owner Alex Behrendt has literally bulldozed new lakes and pools out of virgin soil, adding to the original waters from which the fishery takes its name. Others must have done the same. If their efforts could be multiplied by only a thousand, anglers would have a lot more fishing space —and a lot more security—in this tight little island.

PERMITS AND TRIBAL TERRITORIES

Nine a.m. on a fine autumn day. I was fishing a small stream in the very heart of the Home Counties. Wild plants surrounded me, a veritable jungle of them. Massed reeds bent low over their life-source. The stream, crystal clear, meandered along as if loath to leave this green-tinted beauty behind.

I set up my rod, baited with a worm and flicked the loaded hook to the top of the swim. It carried a few yards in the current before coming to rest on the edge of slack water. I decided to leave it awhile, gathered the line and settled to what promised to be the most delightful trip of the season. Here was peace indeed!

'Have you got a licence?'

Peace, it seemed, was destined to be short-lived. I turned to see the River Authority poised in all its majesty on the bank above and behind me. Unlike the fish from my now empty swim, I had neither time nor the inclination to escape upstream. I did *not* have a licence, and said so honestly enough, explaining that having accepted a last-minute invitation to fish that water I had genuinely overlooked the requirements of local bureaucracy. The Authority proved human enough, but was at pains to emphasise that I was breaking the law. I apologised. I bowed my head in shame. I resolved never to make such a mistake again. And I trembled to think what might have transpired had the RA left its bed that morning from the wrong side.

A free man, I resent laws which allow me to fish my capital river without charge, but demand payment before I may use county waters. I resent still more the situation they create should I dare travel twenty miles without paying further dues in advance. Prosecution, fines, charges for legal representation —all the headaches and heartaches of a court case become grim reality. Such is freedom in the 1960s!

The Bledisloe Report, presented to Parliament in 1961, was in the news recently. Its 151 pages are the end-product of a £4,000 investigation into the Salmon and Freshwater Fisheries Acts. That investigation lasted nearly four years. It will influence governments for decades to come. Paragraph 277 states: 'We have given careful consideration to see whether, for example, by the issue of a national licence valid over the whole of the country on the lines of game and gun licences, the present system could be simplified both for the benefit of anglers and to give greater economy of administration. We have concluded, however, that without a serious interference with the autonomy of river boards and a restriction of their power to raise local revenue to meet essentially local expenditure it is impossible to make such a radical change in the existing structure.'

The advocates of a nation-wide permit have no desire to interfere with the autonomy of river authorities, nor to restrict their financial operations. It is my belief that the Committee did not consider making BOTH types of licence available. In the name of all the salmon in the Dee, why not?

Many enthusiasts travel great distances—matchmen, holiday anglers, businessmen. A national permit would be of inestimable value to them. And no one suffers. The majority, fishing their home waters, will obtain their permits as at present. They will pay no more than at present. And monies raised from the sale of Britain's national licence can surely be apportioned between the various Authorities at the close of each season?

Action by the Minister of Sport might help to bring matters into line with the requirements of the day. Not, I fear, in time for me to benefit, for Whitehall moves as swiftly as the Basingstoke Canal. Even so, I have a stake in this matter . . . My first grandson is due next year!

UNDERWATER GARDENING

Water weeds? The average angler can't abide 'em. He'll walk a mile searching for a bit of clear water rather than fish into a patch of greenstuff. And at the close of the season, when the warmer weather arrives and the weeds are doing a grand job for the fishery—providing cover for eggs and small fry, and breeding beds for a 1,001 different forms of insect life— Mr. Average turns out on a working party and indiscriminately hauls tons of this natural cover on to the banks.

It's a technique known as making new swims. Very satisfying work. It's also an excellent method of playing havoc with life below the surface and reducing the development of a fishery to its absolute minimum.

Bill Keal has written plenty about the value of various aquatic plants, and in this matter I am with him all the way. Fred Wagstaffe has demonstrated more effectively than any other angler I know that it pays to fish for summer and autumn pike with lures skipped across the very heart of heavily weeded shallows. Those pike lie in the weed because they prefer to be there. So do many other species, as Peter Stone has shown us often enough.

Eric Birch, an expert with a life-time's experience of fishery management, has no doubts on this score. In *The Management of Coarse Fishing Waters* (Baker, London, 25s.), Mr. Birch pulls no punches. 'Coarse fish anglers,' he writes, 'seem to be instilled with a violent hatred of water plants or weeds, as they usually prefer to call them. Masses of valuable plants are hauled out of the water annually, and the perpetrators of this action wonder why the fish are small.

'First, the plants provide cover for many species of fish and their wholesale removal exposes the fish to many dangers; in particular pike, winged predators, and of course, man. Second, the plants are usually removed at a time when the insect, mollusc and crustacean population are at their height and consequently much of the food of the fish is removed with the plants.

'The bigger fish migrate to safer surroundings. The smaller fish remain until they have cropped the now-exposed food animals, and then they, too, go in search of other quarters. I often have to recommend the planting of new beds . . . a suggestion never received too kindly, and the mere mention of marginal beds of sedges to act as cover for fishermen, and breeding sites for aquatic insects and animals, sends some people into a frenzy.'

Since many club committees will soon be thinking of ways to improve the fisheries under their control, I'd like to quote an actual case history from a recent issue of *Outdoor Life* in which Ted Janes underlined the importance of weed growth with a long article on pike fishing in New York's Senaca Lake. This water looks as big as anything we have in the Lake District, perhaps bigger. To a Southerner's eye, accustomed to the gravel pits of the Thames Valley, Senaca Lake is a miniature inland sea.

In parts, this venue is as much as 600 ft. deep, and for twenty years or more the pike population has been nothing to write home about. Then in 1960, in a water previously devoid of aquatic plants, milfoil started to grow and spread. Dense jungles of the stuff took hold in marginal waters 2-16 ft. deep. It spread outwards from the shoreline, as much as 100 yards towards the lake centre.

And as the milfoil grew so the pike population exploded. Today, this venue offers some of the finest pike fishing in the area and numbers its stock by the thousand. Why? At Senaca Lake experts found that for many years past the agricultural land around the lake has been fed with artificial fertilisers. Unlike organic manures, these artificials are not totally absorbed by the soil. Chemical traces work through the ground and eventually drain into the water, enriching the bed of the lake and providing the conditions needed for valuable aquatic plants to establish themselves. Obviously, the larger the water the longer this process will take, and at Senaca Lake it had taken quite some time.

What holds good for pike at that New York State venue applies to many fisheries in this country. For 'pike' read tench, carp, roach, rudd or any other species you happen to favour.

Let me close with a thought for that club meeting, the one dealing with work parties and restocking. Instead of spending a bomb on yet another load of fish, why not get a copy of Eric Birch's book, check the plants already in your club waters and create conditions in which the existing stock of fish can breed readily and grow to their maximum size?

You may need a few bags of fertiliser. You may need a selection of plants at present missing from the water. Compare with Mr. Birch the 'weeds' most likely to be of value and spend a fraction of the money, previously debited to restocking policies, on a spot of underwater gardening. It could pay dividends!

THE INLAND FISHERIES TRUST

Go to Ireland for a holiday and you'll need no passport or other documents. There are no currency restrictions, no language barrier. Traffic jams are virtually unknown beyond Dublin and there's not the least problem about crossing the ocean.

You'll find thousands of acres of completely free fishing for brown trout and coarse fish, with no rod licence to pay for. But, and this is a very important 'but', it is not true to say that all Irish fishing is free. Many brown trout waters are preserved by Ireland's angling clubs, most of whom welcome the visitor and charge most reasonably. Other venues are managed, and very well managed, by the Inland Fisheries Trust. These may be fished only by Trust members or by non-members holding a 5s. day ticket.

The Trust operates along the lines of our own National Trust, except that the IFT of Ireland is concerned with water rather than stately homes: with fisheries. Waters under Trust control, for which membership must be paid, are the Midland Lakes of Owel, Ennell, Sheelin, Derravaragh and Glore, in addition to the Little Brosna, Big Brosna, the Inny and Suck river systems and sundry smaller waters in various parts of the country. In the West—on Loughs Corrib, Mask, Conn, Carra and Arrow—the IFT are developing more than 80,000 acres of trout fishing free to all comers.

Day tickets, where needed, are readily available, but full membership at 20s. is usually more economical and the Handbook provides a miscellany of useful maps and general data. This can be arranged before leaving England by writing direct to the Inland Fisheries Trust Incorporated, No. 11 Westmoreland Street, Dublin, 2.

Not all my readers will have the opportunity of a fishing

holiday in Ireland this year, but I fancy that the following notes
—reprinted from a recent report by the IFT—will interest many
English anglers. To my mind, the biggest single factor emerging from a detailed study of the Trust's Annual Report is that
we in Britain have nothing remotely similar: nothing so
practical: nothing to give members across the nation and
beyond the same sense of interest and involvement.

It is hardly surprising that in a country whose pike record stands
at a massive 53 lb., *Esox lucius* is the first fish to be mentioned.*
Irish pike spawn during the period February to April when lake
levels are high or rising and when water temperatures in the
spawning areas reach at least 48-50 deg.F. Spawning is earlier in
some lakes than others, and is earlier during a mild spring than
a cold one. The eggs are deposited in shallow, sheltered situations
where there is a bottom carpet of dead or living vegetation, and
take about 10-14 days to hatch.

The scales of some 12,500 pike from five big limestone lakes and
about 1,000 pike from small lakes have been examined by the
Trust. In Loughs Corrib, Mask, Sheelin, Derravaragh and Ennell
most of the male pike are mature when a year old and the females
when two years old. In small lakes growth is much slower and both
sexes tend to mature a year later than in larger waters.

In general, the growth rate of perch is faster in alkaline than in
neutral or acid waters and is faster in big than in small waters.
Perch tend to become stunted in small lakes, and seriously stunted
where spawning facilities are unlimited but food restricted.

Lakes producing the best quality perch usually have clear water,
fair depths, stony shores and an abundance of crayfish. Very large
perch, 3 lb. or more, may occasionally occur in any water, even
where most of the population are runts, but seldom occur in any
number. These big perch are exceptionally fast-growing individuals
which, as a result of early size advantage over their contemporaries,
probably became predators on sizeable fish, e.g., yearling and two-
year-old perch, while still relatively young themselves.

In the slow-growing populations of perch, growth may virtually
cease after five or six years of age.

Bream spawn in Ireland between Mid-May and Mid-June, at a

* NB: In January 1970, the Irish Specimen Fish Committee announced
its intention of applying 'present rules to past catches'. As a result, John
Garvin's 53-pounder was struck from the list and replaced by a 42 lb. River
Barrow pike caught by Mr. M. Watkins of Muinebeg, Co. Carlow, in 1964.

minimum water temperature of about 60 deg.F. The first food of the fry consists of one-celled algae. Later they feed on water fleas and copepods close to shore. In subsequent seasons, as 'silver bream', they feed more in open water. The adult 'bronze bream' feed mainly on bottom invertebrates and only to a very limited extent, if at all, on plants.

The bream is a long-lived fish and examples up to twenty-three years of age were encountered. It does not become mature until 7-10 years of age. Growth rate is slow. When a year old, the average fork length is only about 1¼ in. Under good conditions Irish bream reach an average length of 16 in. and a weight of 3 lb. at ten years of age. Where food is scarce, however, ten-year-old bream average only about 12 in. in length and 1 lb. 3 oz. in weight. 'Specimen' bream are usually fast-growing individuals from waters where the average growth rate is high, but they are not, as a rule, particularly old fish.

Rudd in Ireland usually spawn from mid-May to early July. The juveniles feed on water fleas and tiny winged insects; the larger rudd on filamentous algae (silkweed), underwater plants and winged insects.

Rudd mature when 3-4 years old. At one year they measure, on average, a little over 1 in. At eight years, under good growing conditions, Irish rudd average 11 in. fork length. Under poor conditions they may measure only 7 in. at eight years and will become severely stunted in small waters.

Growth rates for Rudd x Bream hybrids are intermediate between those of the parent species. In diet, and usually in habits, they resemble rudd rather than bream. Hybrids ripen and shed both milt and eggs, but there is at present no evidence as to whether or not they are fertile *inter se* or with either of the parent species.

In the lower reaches of the Cork Blackwater roach spawn about the end of May, but in the upper reaches of the river spawning is about three weeks later. Growth rates are similar to those of rudd. The diet is in part silkweed and water weeds, and in part crustaceans, molluscs and the young stages of aquatic insects.

Dace spawn from later February to late March, very much earlier than other Irish cyprinids and at a lower water temperature—about 50 deg.F. The eggs are much larger than those of any other cyprinid and are shed on moderately swift, stony shallows.

During the early years of life the growth in length of the dace is considerably faster than that of roach, but the roach, being deeper in the body, becomes the heavier after some years. Dace feed on plants, crustaceans and molluscs, and the young stages of aquatic insects. They also eat large numbers of winged insects.

Finally, the tench. According to the season and the water, they spawn in Ireland from mid-June to late August. They require a minimum water temperature of about 70 deg.F. for spawning, which occurs as a rule during spells of sunny, settled, anticyclonic weather. In some waters and in some years no spawning takes place. It is probably for this reason that tench are less prone to become stunted through over-population in small waters than is the case with rudd, perch or bream.

The tench, like the bream, eats plants only to a limited extent, if at all, the diet of the adult tench being similar to that of bream. They mature at three years and have a shorter life-span than bream. Under good conditions female Irish tench reach a mean length of about 15½ in. and a weight of about 2 lb. 2 oz. at seven years of age. Under poor growing conditions. female tench may average less than 11 in., and weigh only 11 oz., at that age.

MEET TROUBLE HALF-WAY!

Without warning your fishing rights may be endangered. Waters that have never known pollution can suddenly become awash with dead fish. Out of the blue a local authority announces plans that transform a rosy future into no future at all. The committee—indeed, the entire club—face problems that would shake even a highly-organised concern.

The usual thing is to call an emergency meeting, but it's in the lap of the Gods whether those present are remotely capable of coping with the situation. For years, perhaps, members have met and fished and minded their own business. By the very nature of the sport influential contacts elsewhere in the community tend to be neglected. As a result, clubs confronted with such emergencies often feel powerless to do anything but let off steam among themselves and await the inevitable.

It's 1966; we dream dreams of an efficient nation-wide Council. One day they will become reality. A club secretary, faced unexpectedly with a crisis of this kind, will pick up the telephone and discuss matters with highly-qualified staff, able to advise on the immediate situation. The full strength and resources of the Council—financed by you and me and the guys in the next village—will rally behind a group of lads we've never heard of and are never likely to meet. They may live in Newcastle or Merseyside, Llandudno or the Isle of Wight. Does it matter? Next year it could be our turn.

Many regional associations offer at least part of this service. Their officials, experienced and hard-working volunteers, give valuable assistance. But if disaster threatened TODAY would you know what steps to take, what contacts to make? It is not enough to have a vague idea; things move too fast these days. And even when angling has a national administration the Council will have to rely on spirited action and well-informed planning at local level. *Be prepared!* Every club in this country could do worse than make this its motto.

I find it incredible that clubs sharing the same water often have little or no contact; that details of the appropriate association or river authority are not on record; that local councillors and their addresses are unknown. As to the Member of Parliament, his address is more likely to be defined as 'Westminster-I-suppose', and neither police nor local authorities have the foggiest idea of where to contact the club's officials should an emergency arise.

If you find this hard to believe, attend the next club meeting and ask how much of this data IS on record. (After all, the saving or wasting of several hours can mean the difference between a safe fishery and none at all.) The chances are that you will be told to stop worrying and I shall be labelled a bit of an old woman. Be that as it may, few clubs will not benefit by making sure that this kind of information is readily available.

We can no longer function in isolation from the rest of the community. For example, where factory premises border a river or canal stretch it can do no harm for a committee member to introduce himself to the works manager; to ensure that the club secretary's address and phone number are known.

PLATE 15 (*left*) Weighing-in at Buckler's Hard on the Beaulieu river. Bob Pearce hoists the best fish caught in this heat of Southern Television's sea angling championship of 1969. A 50 lb. monkfish, taken aboard a Lymington boat, *The Lily*, it guaranteed its captor a place in the championship finals off Orkney. PLATE 16 (*right*) Dr. Loren Donaldson of Washington University, Seattle, with a 'baby' supertrout—a two-year-old fish. Bred from selected rainbows and their migratory cousins, the American steelhead trout, these fish top 17·5 lb. at three years of age.

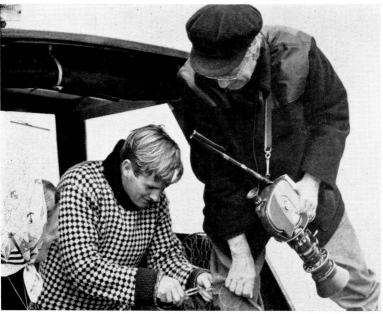

PLATE 17 It happens to the best of us! Unguarded terminal tackle is a menace on a charter boat. Southern TV's cameraman, Stan Brehaut well and truly snagged while filming shots for Jack Hargreaves' 'Out of Town' series.

PLATES 18 & 19 Concentration: the vital factor in competitive angling. *Above,* a winter scene on the Great Ouse—with mile after mile of green umbrellas swept by a hard-biting wind—as Dick Murray of *Angler's Mail* watches his swing-tip for the least sign of action. *Below,* George Hazelgrove fishing off the South Coast; lunch in one hand, the other ready to strike.

The slight trouble involved can be repaid a thousandfold when danger threatens.

Apart from outside contacts, what can be done inside the club at such a time? The entire committee may well be in a state of shock, but they have got to act and act fast. The chances are that certain club members will have specialised knowledge—one will be a solicitor, another an accountant or a surveyor perhaps. Faced with a crisis the question of co-option to the committee should be considered at an early stage. And since co-opted members have no vote unless this is specially given to them, this must be debated at the same time.

Don't hesitate to take your problems to a solicitor if this seems desirable. Your opponents will almost certainly be acting on the instructions of someone no less qualified. Most clubs hesitate to seek legal advice, fearing expenses they can ill-afford. It is true that litigation can cost the earth, but your initial approach will be aimed at gaining expert opinion as to your rights in the matter and an estimate of the action and costs necessary to uphold those rights. The few guineas involved may prove the soundest investment the club ever made!

One of your most valuable allies in time of trouble should be the local Press. Maybe the match results do get tucked away at the foot of page 29: what matters at this crucial moment in the club's history is that your Press Officer and the local reporters are already well acquainted. Believe me, when a news story breaks, the front page of the local Gazette —and that of the County paper—can exert a powerful influence on all manner of people.

TWO LAKES IN WINTER

When I visited Two Lakes that January the surrounding woodlands were as beautiful as ever; clad now in hoar frost, the lakes coated with ice and sparkling in the morning sun; the car park empty. Butch and Lyza, Alex Behrendt's alsatian dogs, gave no sign of recognition. I adjusted the car window and waited for Alex to appear.

'It's OK, John. Come in.' I stayed put. Five yards away, Butch didn't blink an eyelid. Lyza snarled. 'You know it's OK,' I called, 'and I know it's OK. But do they?' Oddly enough, they did. But the fate of anyone foolish enough to poach that water doesn't bear thinking about.

This is when the real work is done at most trout fisheries. Fences to repair, accounts to be sent out for the season ahead, stewponds to be emptied and cleaned. You cannot do much when people are fishing the water every day, and in that respect Two Lakes is a busy spot from April 1 through to September 30.

At the close of each season the trout in the rearing pools are turned out into the lake. The pools are then drained, cleaned out, disinfected with lime and left for at least 6-8 weeks prior to refilling and stocking again in February and March.

Bank trimming was under way when I arrived that day. 'Willows and poplars grow so fast,' Alex told me, 'that even when they are cut back hard it takes only one or two years before they reach the same height again. But plenty of casting space is important.' Even so, cutting back must be done with care if the natural beauty of the fishery is not to be ruined. Alex aims to achieve 'a keepered wilderness'. Leave the odd fallen tree in place, the long-dead and rotted tree stump, and don't clear bankside vegetation so viciously that the wild look is destroyed.

I noted the ice on the water—a solid, thick layer of it. Was he worried about the prospect of winterkill, that loss of fish as ice seals the surface and reduces oxygen supplies? In fact, this is seldom a problem at Two Lakes, and a day or two of icy conditions is nothing to worry about at any fishery. Trouble starts when the ice remains unbroken for a fortnight or more and heavy snowfalls block out the light, preventing the underwater plants from producing oxygen. Trout and pike are the first to suffer.

But if the freeze is short-lived no action of any kind is preferable to smashing the ice with axes or sledge hammers. 'Pike are easily killed by the vibrations set up with an axe,' said Alex. He grinned broadly: 'As much as anglers hate swans, if the birds really like a lake and refuse to leave it, always remember that they contribute something to the fishery by keeping the water open in winter.' Not that swans are needed at Two Lakes. The risk of winterkill is overcome by opening the hatches and lowering the water level. This leaves a gap of several inches between the surface of the lake and the underside of the ice layer. The ice eventually cracks and breaks-up out in the middle, and when that happens at night it's like a bomb going off. Oddly enough, the vibrations that sets up seem to have no ill effects on the fish.

Seventy rods fished Two Lakes last season, recording a total catch of 4,903 trout averaging 2 lb. 6½ oz. Of those 4,903 fish, one was a 7-pounder, four were 6-pounders, 23 scaled 5 lb. and 179 were 4-lb.-plus. More than 1,000 of the remainder weighed 3 lb. or more.

One of the biggest problems facing owners of shallow-water lakes, and many an angling club for that matter, is weed control. Labour rates are high and the amount that can be cut and cleared by hand in one day is not very great. Alex explained how he copes with milfoil and Canadian pondweed. No chains or cutters: just polythene and patience.

He was the first fishery owner in Britain to use black polythene sheeting for this purpose. Each sheet measures 16 yds.

by 8 yds. and can be handled by two men in all but the windiest conditions. Cost, around £5 each. Weighted with stones at the four corners, or tied to stakes driven into the bed of the lake, these sheets block out the light and ensure a 100 per cent weed kill—even water lilies.

The sheets are put down in January. By April the covered areas are weed-free and the polythene can be towed to the next patch. If desired, it can be left in position all the year around, either at the surface or anchored on the bed of the lake.

At Two Lakes, black polythene has been in use for the past five years. 'The initial cost was no more than normal labour charges for that year. After all this time it probably costs no more than one shilling for every patch cleared of weed.' (*See Plate 7.*)

Where fisheries are concerned, Alex Behrendt is an expert —one of the few and certainly one of the best in Britain today. He was fish farming in Norway before the 1939-45 war and his personal experience includes the rearing of carp, tench and shellfish, in addition to his beloved trout. I asked him to give me one important tip that I could pass on to any club or syndicate thinking of stocking a trout water in the season ahead.

Alex thought for a moment. 'You have to remember,' he said, 'that every fishery is different in one way or another. But if you want to discover what class of fish a lake is capable of producing, let the fish tell you. Stock with trout of one size only. Whatever else you do, *don't* put sixty per cent of one size, ten per cent two inches larger and so on. By the end of that year they'll be so mixed up you won't know what you've got. But if they are all five-inch trout to start with, there can be no argument when it comes to assessing the water's potential. Whether they are then thirteen inches or six inches, or somewhere between those extremes, you have a perfect guide to growth rates and the water's natural food stocks can either be improved or left accordingly.'

I nodded at Butch. 'That sounds good,' I said. And to my astonishment, he wagged his tail!

SIXTY-SECOND KNOCKOUT

If at first sight and without a single trip of the tongue you can pronounce 'meta-aminobenzoic acid ethylester' you're a better man than I am. Its trade name, MS-222, is far less a mouthful. This synthetic substance is the most efficient fish anaesthetic yet produced. It will knock out a 400 lb. shark in 60 seconds or prepare fingerling trout for a journey across the globe.

The French newspaper, *La Patrie*, told how live trout, salmon and other species, were first packed in water treated with MS-222 and then mailed from Canada to Paris. The method used on that occasion should interest the NAC's research sub-committee concerned with striped bass. With each female producing 500,000 eggs we are not likely to need many stockfish, and if live salmon can be shipped over, so can 'stripers'.

The fish needed in Paris were despatched from the University of Montreal, each one sealed in a plastic bag containing a solution of one part MS-222 to 10,000 parts of water. Oxygen was pumped in so that the pressure inside the bags equalled the atmospheric pressure; the fish could utilise the oxygen and the inflated bags served to protect them during their journey. They were placed in a refrigerated container with a temperature of 1-2 deg.C. (35 deg.F.) and mailed via commercial airlines to Paris where they were revived by being tipped into fresh water.

One of Japan's largest airlines carries more fish than people from South East Asia to Europe, and the pick of their passengers are treated with MS-222 before leaving the ground. The drug was discovered by Maurice Sandoz during his search for a reliable substitute for cocaine. It is made by Sandoz Ltd. of Balse, Switzerland, and used almost entirely in research work with fish and other cold-blooded creatures, and in fishery management.

MS-222 is supplied in powder form. It can be mixed with fresh or saltwater in concentrations ranging from 1:500 to 1:30,000 or more, the 'mix' varying with the job in hand. A record porbeagle shark could be anaesthetised within one minute with a 1:1,000 seawater solution. That's a level tea-spoonful in approximately four and a half pints of water.

The procedure involved is really very simple: no question of plunging hypodermics into sharks anxious to be about their business. The research angler interested in sharks, conger, tope, skate, monkfish and other lethal species has only to bring his fish alongside and its head above water while a colleague sprays the anaesthetic on to its gills and mouth, using a water pistol or garden syringe. Within fifteen seconds the drug starts to work. Within one minute the fish will be completely immobilised.

It can then be lifted aboard—either tailed in or cradled in a net suspended from the side of the boat—tagged, measured or photographed, and released. Once in the water the fish should be held to the boat until it recovers, and this may take 5-30 minutes, according to the size of the fish and the strength of the solution employed.

Smaller species may be anaesthetised by lowering them into a container of treated water and removing the hook when the drug has taken effect. Fish so treated can be eaten with safety—no special precautions are necessary before cooking them.

MS-222 has obvious advantages in fish photography, not least that such fish will lie still. Close-ups are possible without risk and with minimum wastage of film. I agree that any species can be made to lie still with the help of the 'clonker' carried by all competent charter skippers. But where photography is the aim clonkers are anything but ideal. Dead fish soon lose the colour values displayed in life: drugged fish do not.

Using MS-222 in concentrations of 1:1,000 on a variety of

species, a leading researcher reports that within two minutes the chromatophores or colour cells expand to reveal maximum brilliance. After a few more minutes under the anaesthetic fish display their darkest tones as the melanophores—cells housing a dark pigment called melanin—expand to their maximum and reduce the intensity of neighbouring yellow, red and silver-hued cells.

Clubs facing the problem of moving large specimens over considerable distances should find MS-222 a splendid ally. The fish moved will need less water and consume far less oxygen than those transported in the usual way.

When tagging, weighing, measuring or checking the condition of fish this drug enables fisheries or club personnel to work faster, more easily and with negligible risk to the stock handled by them. Even as a tranquilliser it has possibilities for freshwater angling. Tests have established that anaesthetised trout dropped from aircraft flying ninety feet above the surface suffered no damage. The principle has other applications. For example, it may be premature to suggest that a dip in MS-222 should precede the weighing-in of match-caught fish. But drugged fish don't leap from the scales or try to swim in mid-air. They come to no harm and they recover quickly when returned to the water. If the National Federation of Anglers is really concerned about damage to its roach, dace and bream stocks, experiments along these lines warrant serious consideration.

I REMEMBER WHEN THE RUSHES GREW!

The fish with a name reminiscent of a Welsh railway station —*Ctenopharyngodon idella*—must live five to nine years before reaching sexual maturity. It rarely breeds outside its native rivers and they are on the other side of the world. But let us hope that no one will gamble too heavily on the discouraging effects of the English climate, for the creature in question is the white amur—the grass-eating carp.

These facts and others, part of the most interesting scientific paper to come my way for some time, have just been reprinted from the Journal of Fish Biology, published by the Fisheries Society of the British Isles.* The author, D. G. Cross of the Salmon and Freshwater Fisheries Laboratory, London, mentions the superficial resemblance between the grass carp and our native chub. As a matter of fact, both fish belong to the same order, Cypriniformes, but apart from a similar body shape the relationship is somewhat distant.

Mr. Cross describes the grass carp as having a slightly elongated body, a relatively large head and mouth, and upper parts of an olive brown. The lower parts of its body are of a silver hue. That the mouth is large need surprise no one; behind it lurks the most ravenous appetite in the kingdom of freshwater fishes. If eating contests were held below the surface the grass carp would win every time. At the warmest period of the year this fish devours more than its own weight of plant material every day.

In order to tear away the aquatic green stuff on which it lives, the grass carp is equipped not only with powerful pharyngeal teeth, but with a horny pad set in the roof of the pharynx. Plants gripped between this pad and the pharyngeal bones are torn free by violent movements of the fish's body. Most herbivores have a long gut relative to their body length, but in this underwater mowing machine the gut is unusually short— about one-fifth the length that might be expected—making the grass carp a most inefficient digester of greenstuffs. Indeed, its faeces contain about fifty per cent unused, undigested food. As a result, the fish devours about twice the quantity of greenfood it would otherwise need. Failing this, it could not extract sufficient nourishment to maintain life at this high level of wastage.

* *Aquatic Weed Control using Grass Carp*, by D. G. Cross. J.Fish.Biol. (1969)1. pp. 27-30.

In water temperatures below 10 deg.C. (50 deg.F.) it is a very selective eater, cropping only the most tender plants. But as the temperature hots up so does its yen for fresh salads. Becoming less and less selective, the carp munches its merry way through all kinds of vegetation, including the toughest of rushes. The water lily is, I believe, one of the few plants known to be carp-proof.

It is this weed-eating activity that so endears the fish to the Ministry and to River Authorities. The latter spend about £1¼-million on weed clearance every year—enough to make the grass carp an ally of great potential. But, say the Ministry, the numbers of grass carp must be controlled. Mr. Cross makes the point: 'There is a remote possibility that the fish will breed in this country, and it would be unthinkable to introduce a species which would breed uncontrollably and become a nuisance.' To which, no doubt, every roach angler along the Great Ouse Relief Channel will respond, 'And zanders to you, too!'

But the final, serious note from this official source should go on record within reach of future anglers. 'The fish,' writes Mr. Cross, 'must not upset the habitat to the detriment of existing species of fish. The drainage engineer would be content if the grass carp ate all the water weed in a river, but the native fish species would suffer considerably since the weeds harbour much of their food and provide suitable spawning sites.

'Thus it will be important to determine the density at which a water will have to be stocked with grass carp to control the weeds to the satisfaction of the drainage engineer and yet to provide conditions under which existing fish species will continue to flourish. This problem will be much simplified should it be that the grass carp will not breed in this country. At the present time it appears that there will be no insurmountable problems attached to the introduction of grass carp to this country, but tests will have to be performed here before any decision on the use of this fish can be taken.'

In another three to seven years (1972-1976) we shall all be

in a position to judge whether problems exist or not. For that is when Britain's grass carp are due to spawn for the first time!

SACRED COWS

The need for improved fishery management is becoming increasingly evident. Whether club water, River Authority or private fishery, every venue in the land must be made to provide better sport for still more anglers. In the years 1966-67 the National Association of Specimen Groups did much to foster a fresh approach to this aspect of coarse angling. Active participation in research programmes; the publication of data via press articles and private circulars; the marshalling of information that has existed for years unbeknown to the layman— these and other activities have produced knowledge of great practical value.

Progressive local clubs and regional associations have long co-operated with experts in this field to improve and extend existing fisheries, create new ones and turn fourth-rate venues into waters to be proud of. This is twentieth-century angling! It is a solution, in part at least, to water shortages and the ever-increasing demand for club membership. As yet, too few coarse fisheries are involved. In terms of sound management many have progressed very little beyond the stewponds of the Dark Ages. Indeed, many a stewpond was better stocked!

For the vast majority, 'management' means work parties. As a rule, these represent only a fraction of the membership. They turn out during the close season, and what do they accomplish. Overhangs and awkward branches are cut back. Last season's litter is cleared away. And that—thank goodness!— is the end of fishery management for another year. Restocking? Sooner or later a pit will be filled in or surplus fish offered by another club. No one will think to question the food supplies, the quality and well-being of the new stock. Fish need water and water you've got. Dump 'em in!

At venues teeming with stunted roach and perch little or no effort is made to produce Grade 'A' specimens. A few pike may be introduced to gobble up the surplus, which is asking an awful lot of Mother Nature. Someone might even propose that a hundred or so of these wretched midgets be offered to the club down the road. But no one will have the good sense to suggest getting rid of them—netting them out in their thousands. Whatever else happens, the fish must be preserved. Sacred cows of India!

Stunted, diseased or starving, it matters not. These fish are governed by the coarse angler's creed, THOU SHALT NOT KILL. It just doesn't register that fishery management and fish farming are one and the same. A good farmer culls his stock, ruthlessly, or goes bankrupt.

Coarse angling today wallows in the slushy sentimentality of the city-bred naturalist. Because of this, acres of potentially fine water are fourth-rate and worse. I know fisheries—as you may—where sound management dictates only one course of action. Remove the entire stock; let the water lie fallow for a season or two; introduce fertilisers and plan the plant, insect and other underwater life. Then, and only then, will those waters be fit to receive top-quality stock in quantity. But within a very short time the sport provided could exceed the wildest dreams of those who spend their days yanking out, weighing and putting back tiddlers!

TAPEWORM—HERE TO STAY

I sat beside a keen roach angler at a pit in the Thames Valley. 'We've got a lot of diseased fish,' he said, 'Tapeworm—that's our plague. It doesn't bother us any more than it bothers the fish, but I'd rather be without it.' With that his float dipped.

He struck and a fish was on; a roach of about six ounces. Sure enough, there was the typical tapeworm bulge in the forward end of its underside.

Most experienced anglers would have recognised the tapeworm symptom immediately, certainly those fishing London waters, yet not one in fifty has ever seen this most common of parasitic worms. Does it bother the fish? I leave you to form your own conclusion when you have read this article. The next time you net a heavily infected roach, kill it and slit open the body cavity: examine this parasite for yourself.

There are many different tapeworms. The Latin name for this one is *Ligula intestinalis*. *Ligula* means, quite simply, a small tongue, which is for all the world what these creatures look like—white, elongated tongues! They vary in length from half an inch to something approaching three feet, possibly more.

The second part of their Latin name gives a further clue. *Intestinalis*. A tongue-shaped creature living in the intestine of its host. At least, that's where it first sets up home inside the fish. Eventually, the worm breaks through the wall of the intestine and continues its development within the body cavity.

But how do they get there in the first place? My friend at the pit asked the same question. I pointed to a flock of gulls quarrelling over a carcase floating many yards out. A pair of crested grebes were active in mid-water, and a few moments later a heron flew over with that slow, majestic wing beat. Had we been on the Great Ouse, as I was a few weeks ago, my friend would have seen a kingfisher studying the water from an overhanging willow tree. These and many other birds have one thing in common: they eat fish. And when they make a meal of an infected fish the worms go too!

Strictly speaking, that is the final phase in the life cycle of the tapeworm, for within the bird's intestine *Ligula* lays its eggs and dies. The life-pattern starts all over again.

Mixed with the bird's droppings, the tapeworm eggs return to the water. They hatch as minute larvae within a few days, microscopic creatures able to move freely in the water. In order to continue the life cycle these larvae must be eaten by a certain type of plankton. Within a fortnight, and still inside the host plankton, the tiny tapeworm changes into a more advanced larval form.

Now comes another hazard. The plankton housing the tapeworm larva must be swallowed by a fish before further development can take place. Vast numbers of these larvae are said to be destroyed by the stomach acids of their second host—usually roach—but enough survive to reach the intestine and change, yet again, into small but perfectly formed tapeworms.

To what extent do they harm fish and sport? These worms lie with very little movement inside the body cavity. In fact, the body of the fish grows to an abnormal shape specially to accommodate them! But they do great damage by putting pressure on the internal organs, forcing them into unnatural positions and limiting their function. The tapeworm also makes full use of food juices digested by the fish. And as the worm develops—or rather, 'worms', for though single parasites are commonly found there can be twenty or more in one fish—it robs its host to the point at which malnutrition, stunted growth and sub-standard health are inescapable.

In the final stages, a year or more after the fish sucked in the infected zooplankton, the fish's internal organs cease to function effectively and the fish becomes sterile.

A different tapeworm infestation occurs in sticklebacks. This is known as *Schistocephalus*. It develops as a larva inside the fish and changes to the adult worm only when it reaches the intestine of its final host, a fish-eating bird.

In his book, *A History of Fishes*, J. R. Norman notes that in Italy and Southern France *Ligula* is considered a delicacy and appears on restaurant menus as 'Maccaroni piatti' and 'Ver blanc' respectively. Thank you, but I would rather go hungry.

Can anything be done to improve matters on infected waters? At this stage, nothing. As usual with fish diseases, too little research has been carried out—far too little to indicate effective controls outside a laboratory tank. On the face of it, total elimination is impossible. From bird to water, to zooplankton, to fish, to bird. You cannot wipe out the birds, there are too many of them and they do much good in other ways. You cannot kill the plankton, it's a vital food source of the very fish you are trying to protect. It seems that in our lifetime at least we must accept the inevitable . . . the tapeworm is here to stay!

SALTWATER CARP

There can be very few natural waters left to us, by which I mean waters totally unaffected by Man's influence. No pesticides drain into them, no remnants of fertilisers from adjoining fields. No abstraction lowers the water level and no one interferes with the fish, their cover or the many sources of food above- and below-water.

Our fisheries today are far more artificial than we care to think. And that being so, we are involved to one degree or another in farming those waters: for sport, not food. All too often we give Nature the very minimum of assistance and leave her to make the best of it. Then we moan like cats on a tin roof because the fishing is not what it was. The truth is that if our farming techniques are hopelessly inadequate, as I think they are, the sport produced must be correspondingly poor.

The idea of farming for top-quality angling has yet to catch on with coarse fishermen. It will. As the concrete jungles spread we shall have no alternative. Only in this way can the gradual deterioration of our waters—the disease level and the reduced quality of fish stocks—be halted and the trend reversed. Then, no doubt, we shall wonder why we failed to appreciate the possibilities years earlier, for the end-product will be angling of such quality that the popularity of the sport will outstrip all others by a far greater margin than it does now.

It's time we started thinking, and acting. No one is going to make the transition for us. From Hungary to Hong Kong fish culture is utilising existing waters and creating new ones. The commercial production of coarse fish—carp, bream, zander and other species—is big business. For some countries it forms an important part of their national economy and their achievements are such as to make our stunted roach and perch something to be ashamed of. Sub-standard stocks are not to be tolerated when you farm for your living.

Fish foods, weed growth, oxygen supplies and the mineral content of the water must all balance or be made to balance if the finest possible crop is to be taken. Breeding stock must be of the highest quality. It isn't difficult. Why in heaven's name shouldn't the same principles hold good for every still-water fishery in England?

I see from a report in *The Times* that a saltwater fish farm is to operate off the Cornish coast, the first in Britain to raise fish from the egg to the table. The news reminds me of another pet theory, one which could provide fine sport right now. If our towns and cities continue to spread then by AD 2000 we may have to give it a trial.

In many coastal areas marsh or wasteland—ground that may stand idle for another century or more—could be acquired at rock-bottom prices by local clubs and bulldozed into fisheries for stock of this kind. The grey mullet is one species to be raised in the Cornish venture. Mullet, like flounders, thrive in salt, brackish or near-fresh water. They will not breed in captivity, but they grow, fast. And on light tackle they are great sportfish.

Mullet and flounder are the obvious choice for seawater venues, but at some sites the degree of salinity could be controlled by tapping freshwater drains or by creating new ones. Carp, zander, pike, perch and other species are potential stock in fisheries that do not have too high a salt content.

One fine day I hope to visit Henry Khan at the paper's Paris office and drive with him across France to a little place called Arcachon, south-west of Bordeaux. Not for its fine beach or its world-famous oyster farm. At Arcachon they have the breeding of mullet organised to perfection.

Look at any map of France and you will see the estuary of the River Leyre forming a brackish-water lagoon just above the town. What you will not see on your map are the attractive ponds between the tidal shores of the lagoon and the surrounding agricultural land. Sea-dykes keep the highest tides from swamping these man-made pools—wide, earthen walls in which the French have built double sluice gates, each one separated from its twin by a gap of only a few yards. That gap between the seaward gate and the pond gate is the key to re-stocking these fisheries.

In the spring when the mullet fry shoal in the lagoon, the gate nearest the sea is fully opened at low water while its twin adjoining the pond is raised sufficiently to set a gentle flow of water running from the pond, through the space between the two sluices and out into the estuary. The mullet fry gather in their hundreds at this outlet and swim along the current it creates, into the gap between the sluices. When sufficient fry have assembled, the seaward gate is closed and the inner gate opened wide until the water reaches the same level as the pond. At that point the mullet swim into the ponds. With the minimum of trouble and expense another year's supply of fish starts the long journey to the tables of France.

Prawns provide a valuable second crop in many waters organised along these lines. Now if the French, Italians, Americans, Taiwans, Israelis, Cambodians and a host of other races can do this for food—many of them with much simplified versions of the brackish lakes at Arcachon—what is to stop us from establishing some of the finest sport fisheries in the world using the same techniques? Heaven knows, we have enough coastline doing nothing!

Think, before you write off the idea, of the thousands of new and relatively inexpensive venues we could create. Given suitable ground, it's not so zany to consider pumping water from the sea into cliff-top lakes or ponds. And if sufficient freshwater can be obtained to reduce salinity—as it can be at many potential sites—top-class mixed fisheries can be brought within reach of thousands whose only sport at present is that provided by the open sea.

OPERATION BIG FISH

A Boeing 707 took off for Japan. Seconds later a Caravelle taxied the first 200 yards towards Paris. But I hadn't come to London Airport to watch the planes go by. I parked the car and turned into the clubroom of BEA's Silver Wings Club where Alec Viner, secretary of the Angling Society, had arranged a special showing of a film covering the last days of what had once been the finest stillwater fishery in the South-East—Moor Lane, near Staines.

Chairman Reg Muncey introduced me to many of the anglers who featured in the Moor Lane story. And as the projector was switched on he said with a broad grin, 'I shan't be in tomorrow. My back "goes" every time I see this film!'

The film runs for nearly an hour—an hour of surprises, disappointments and successes spanning two years of effort and laughter, hard slog and almost bloody-minded determination. It culminates in the rescue of at least 100,000 fish and the birth of a new fishery. In cash terms the tench alone were valued at between £7,500 and £11,000 on current market prices. Many of those fish weighed from 6¼ lb. to 8-lb.-plus. Some of the roach could by now have reached record-breaking proportions. Not isolated specimens: dozens of them!

But let's go back to the beginning of the story; to a day in February, 1964. Silver Wings had ruled this fishery since 1958, knowing that it had been scheduled as an emergency reservoir more than twenty years earlier. Season after season the club fished as though nothing could ever change the sport in that tree-lined setting. Notice to quit came like a bolt out of the blue.

One minute they were leaseholders of a superb venue; the next they stared aghast at a printed message that left no room for doubt and no hope of reprieve. They had twelve months to get out. At the end of that time their clubhouse would be demolished, their two lakes drained, empty. Of utmost concern was the fact that they had no other venue, either for their members or the vast shoals sheltering in those 150 acres of water.

You may think I exaggerate the quality of sport enjoyed by BEA's angling club, but how else can one write of such a place? Match records show roach of 2-lb.-plus, tench to 6¼ lb. and rudd weighing 2 lb. 5 oz. There were crucians and perch between two and three pounds each and their pike record was a hefty 28½-pounder. Archie Aldridge, the club's first secretary, weighed-in more than 400 lb. of fish in one season, and bags of tench in excess of 50 lb. were commonplace. It was super-fishing with a vengeance!

With notice to quit, no one was quite sure what to do next. Not one member of the committee had any specialised knowledge of fishery management or knew the cod end from the wing of a net. They voted to build and put down traps, and gave hundreds of fish to neighbouring clubs as their own committeemen travelled the country in search of a new water, without success. But trapping proved far too slow. Draining operations were under way and the water level was falling steadily. The rescue of those thousands of fish became virtually a crusade, the No. 1 reason for living, for the twelve men who formed the hard core of the working party.

Their wives were the heroines of the Moor Lane saga as month in and month out, the men laboured until no daylight was left. Their clothes stank of fish and mud; their meals were often left untouched because they were too tired to eat anything.

Realising that if they lacked knowledge there must be those who could help, the committee contacted Dr. Charles Franklin. It was the best move they could have made. Following Dr. Franklin's advice, things started to happen. Nets, boats and frogmen went into action. Sweep after sweep ended with the

15 ft. bag and both wings stuffed with fish—with tench and roach, perch and crucian carp. One or two chub were netted, the heaviest a four-pounder, and their best tench scaled 8 lb. 9 oz.

Other waters benefited as the fish were distributed in their thousands, but at long last a new Silver Wings fishery was found. That, more than anything else, put fresh heart into the rescuers. They 'stored' selected specimens in an ornamental pond and turned a cooling tank at London Airport into a gigantic aquarium, packed with fish.

But the stocks didn't always come that easily. There was the day when a routine sweep produced an exceptional catch. In baths, bins and buckets—anything that would hold fish— they were hauled up the steep and slippery banks and the big tanks carefully loaded on to a lorry. The driver was given the OK to move off. His vehicle lurched forward a couple of feet and stopped, with a puncture. Every one of those fish had to be unloaded, carried back down the banks and replaced no less carefully in the fast-falling water. A precious day's effort, wasted.

But there were unexpected catches to offset the heartaches, among them a Post Office safe stuffed with dog and TV licences. That earned the club an award of £10 from the Postmaster-General. More safes came to light, adding to the incredible total of 200 tons of old iron of every shape imaginable.

There was the afternoon when the first phosphor bombs were drawn in. During the war Moor Lane had been part of a Commando training ground. Now those bombs exploded— 'harmlessly enough', said Bill Slator, fisheries officer and slave-driver-in-chief—within minutes of reaching the air. But harmless or not, some found them too close for comfort!

And there were the unfortunate shoppers in Uxbridge who stared pop-eyed from the pavements at a 4 lb. pike flapping its tail in the middle of the High Street. They were not to know it had jumped from its bin and slithered from the lorry disappearing into the distance.

From start to finish, the Metropolitan Water Board and

their contractors gave every co-operation. Fortunately for Silver
Wings, the contract ran beyond the expected timing to give
nearly two years in which to set traps, electro-fish and net the
stock out. Offers of help from other clubs did much to boost
morale—both equipment and volunteer labour had it been
needed. In fact, on those steep banks more than twelve men
would have been an embarrassment.

Inevitably, many good fish were left behind as that fine
venue was reduced to a series of mud-rimmed puddles. In the
closing stages Moor Lane looked more like the craters of the
moon, but by then one of the biggest rescue operations ever
staged by a small club had been completed.

A few miles away, the new fishery was shaping up well,
stocked with specimens most of us would rate the fish of a
lifetime. By any standards the saving of 100,000 prime fish
must be considered a major triumph for all concerned. It's a
story I've been happy to tell; a story which has never appeared
in print before. As the film ended that night at London Airport, Brian Davies, scales officer for Silver Wings AS, had the
last word.

'I'd like to see that film in reverse,' he said. 'We'd be putting
the fish back again—and the water!'

PART FIVE

SALTWATER

BIG BASS AT A BANQUET

'There was this pig,' said Old Tom as his red-painted dinghy carried us out of Kinsale Harbour and up-river on the first day of my holiday. 'It was dead—lying half in the water, half on the shore. And nuzzling at its open stomach were five of the biggest bass I've ever seen in my life.'

Tom White knows more about bass in that part of Ireland than any man alive. He ought to; for years he has fished that beautiful estuary, almost daily, from spring through to late autumn. I envy very few men. Tom, with his 12 ft. boat moored in front of the Trident Hotel, is one of them. And if you wonder at my reference to 'Old' Tom let me add that he served with the Argyle and Sutherland Highlanders before the first world war. His army number has just two numerals —76.

Kinsale has become famous for its deep sea fishing and the many facilities provided by the Angling Centre so ably managed by Peggy Green. In fact, it has much more to offer than giant skate, ling and shark, and the wrecks and rocks miles out from land. For the freshwater enthusiast seeking fishing with a difference, this spot is 'a natural'. According to the season, you'll see salmon and sea trout leaping from the water as they head up the River Bandon. They leap all day and much of the night. And without going near the open sea you may catch conger, skate, gurnard, pollack, plaice, mullet, doggies, mackerel and codling. And, of course, bass.

Which brings us back to the dead pig.

Over the noise of the outboard engine and the rippling water caressing the boat's hull, Tom told me how on that occasion he could hardly believe the evidence of his one good eye. Like any other angler, his mind was working overtime. How best to lure those monster bass from their grisly banquet?

183

Spinning is Tom's specialty. It works well for him. In one season he logged 604 bass, casting from his boat and from various shore marks along the banks and bays of the tidal stretch. So, 50 yds. down-river of the big fish he tied on a German sprat, started the 3½ hp motor and turned against the tide in a wide arc across the estuary, aiming to get above the fish without disturbing them and then drift down again and gently, very gently, drop anchor.

With a chuckle he told me that for once his luck was in. 'I cast beyond those five bass and played the lure as close to the carcase as I dare. And I played it with my heart in my mouth!' First cast, nothing.

Tom rammed his black beret even more firmly on to his head and cast again, alert for the least sign of action as the lure moved through the clear, shallow water. He watched its flickering glint as it neared the pig; saw the largest of the five fish drift out, half turn and pause. Then it went for the sprat with all the speed it could muster, and Tom's solid glass rod, a lightweight six-footer, bent hard over under the strain.

'There was no time for prayers. I sent an SOS to the Almighty and played that fish as I've never played a fish before. It fought like a demon.'

Demon or not, it was brought to the net—there's never a gaff in Tom White's boat—and Tom just sat there staring at this gigantic, silvery creature, a veritable prince of its kind.

He could not recall how long he sat there, but above him towered the broad rock faces guarding this sector of Kinsale's estuary, the great crevices moss-grown and tinted with sea pinks. Higher up, the steep green fields almost run over the edge as earth and rock meet, producing a galaxy of colour as bluebells, white London pride and the silver-green of new bracken mingles with the yellows and golds of Irish gorse in bloom.

Anchored out from the seaweed-covered rocks below, Tom killed his fish and reached for the spring balance. The needle juddered: registered 13¼ lb. Quite a catch, even for a man who at one time held the garfish record and had come very close with several others.

For once in his life Tom White did not fish on. He lit a cigarette, lifted the anchor and took yet another look at the big bass. Then, with a tug at the starter cord, he hefted life into the outboard motor and headed back along that sun-capped waterway to the Trident Hotel. In midstream the sea-trout must have jumped, wriggled in mid-air and jumped still higher. I don't suppose Tom saw or heard them. And with a 13¼ lb. bass on the floor of the boat I doubt if you would have seen them either!

TIE ME A FLY!

Remember that old song title, 'Where do all the flies go—in the wintertime?' It's pre-war vintage, but in the years between I've found the answer.

Many a traditional trout fly stays in service for much of the winter, searching out grayling along the bright waters. Some provide sport for perch fishers on the big reservoirs. Still more are plied on backwaters and sheltered lakes where rudd and roach abound. But the majority, sad to relate, are rested until another trout season comes round. Many a fisherman whiles away the winter evenings making good the gaps in his fly box, for the man who can fish through a successful season without casualties is either dead lucky, excessively cautious, or both.

Not that I make any claims as a dresser of flies. I tie a wet fly of doubtful pedigree and can fashion nymphs, simple but effective, from tufts of seal fur. Heaven knows which of the underwater families these hairy killers resemble, but they must be first cousin to something or other. Rainbows, perch, grayling, sea and brown trout have all shown their appreciation.

One of these days I must become an expert; take a course in fly tying and develop this crude economy into the art form practised by members of the Fly Dressers' Guild. Not that traditional patterns interest me in the slightest. But unorthodox dressings do. Indeed, I have a sneaking suspicion that if the

FDG and others were a little less conservative fly-fishing would feature far more than it does at many venues today. It is the ultimate technique where sport and sense of contact with the fish are prime considerations.

The use of light tackle from boat and beach already heralds a new phase in saltwater angling, but not so long ago a beach rod weighing 2½ lb. was thought to be the perfect weapon. Today, an 11-footer of just 16 oz. does the same job, gives greater sport and is no strain to hold from dawn to dusk or *vice versa*. The light boat rods we now use would have been laughed to scorn a few years back. But they catch fish, good fish, every week of the year.

There is, too, that in-between type of angling confined to the estuaries, of interest to all who refuse the direct transition from coarse to sea or game fishing. For whether you spin or bait-fish, light tackle ensures fine sport on these waters and there's a sense of quiet sadly lacking at many popular freshwater venues. In all this, specialised forms of fly-fishing could be the next major development.

I am convinced that in the years ahead more and more of us will turn towards fly and feather fishing, experimenting with methods that a few pioneers have already proved effective. Don't ask me where to draw the line between feathers and the true 'fly', unless it be that the fly is a precise imitation of a living creature and feathers anything that you and the fish care to make them.

If imitation matters at all, it does not seem logical to suppose that its advantages are confined to trout fishing. But have you ever tried to match a living squid, brit, prawn, sandeel or cuttle-fish? Think how killing such dressings could be when fish are 'mad on' one particular type of food. Who knows, by 1975 the Silvery Sprat may be as important as the Sherry Spinner!

For that matter, have you ever thought to tie a fly resembling a mackerel? In the summer of 1969 Mike Prorok of Northampton did just that. If memory serves me right, he used 8/o's in tandem and mauve, white and pink feathers to provide lures ranging from 6-10 in. long.

His quarry? ... Shark!

It was, I believe, the first attempt ever made in Britain to take porbeagle shark on fly. On several other occasions that summer Mike could have had a whale of a time off the Isle of Wight. Porbeagle came so close to the boat we could have hand-fed the brutes. But the weekend that he spent with Dick Downes, Trevor Prince and myself everything was against us. Air and water temperatures fell; the mackerel on which the shark feed went deep and the shark went with them, far beyond the range of Mike's heavy-duty saltwater fly-gear.

Dick Downes confirmed that he gets a high proportion of shark runs on his mackerel feathers—trace and shark soon parting company! It gives some indication of the scope that exists for the angler ready and willing to experiment.

If feathering and fly-fishing are closely related, F. W. Holiday's fascinating book, *Feathering for Sea Fish* (published by Herbert Jenkins) comes close to marrying the two. As an introduction to the art, and to such allied subjects as the feeding habits and seasonal movements of various fishes, this little volume is hard to beat. The author deals with the open sea, estuaries and inlets, and with techniques paying dividends in these waters. Here, too, is virgin territory for the man who will tie his own lures and who knows how and when to use them.

I was reminded of this while fishing Christchurch Harbour one autumn day with John Harvey of Taunton. We watched shoals of minnow-like fish massing in the shallows; fish with a peculiar little hump just behind the head. Taken from the water, each one had a scintillating dark blue band along its back. They were bass, about 1½-2 in. long. That same day John caught the smallest bass I've ever seen on rod and line. It measured just under 2in., and fell for a maggot, floatfished on a size 10 hook. And that was a big fish compared with the thousands of little fellows frequenting the more sheltered margins.

Big fish, they say, eat little fish. So what preyed on those bass-lings? Sea-trout, perhaps? Or was it still bigger bass? Was it mullet, since mullet there take spinners so readily? I don't know, but I would have given a lot for a lure matching those small-fry, just to find out. It would take a fair degree of skill to produce anything quite so unorthodox and I do not suppose that there's a shop in the land with such patterns in stock. (See Plate 11.)

Pike flies, bass flies, cod and shark flies; mullet, mackerel and conger flies—the list is a long one and the prospect intriguing. Or would you prefer to class them all as feathers and insist that any old thing will do?

HAVE THE TUNNY RETURNED?

For many boat-owners along the South and West Coasts this summer there has been only one fish in the sea. It may be labelled porbeagle, blue or thresher. Some talk of mako, with their fingers crossed. But the fish is always the same: shark. Hundreds of anglers are praying for an early start to the 1969 cod season. 'Anything,' said a friend of mine, 'anything at all to get the skipper's mind off man-eaters!' Not that the cod season will necessarily close the shark saga. It's my guess that the more daring hunters will roam far afield, and late, in search of the retreating mackerel shoals and the sharks moving with them.

Up North they have no big-game species—yet. But there is a persistent and exciting whisper along the NE coast. The tunny, they say, are back in numbers, sighted by Grimsby trawlermen far out in the North Sea.

It is just 15 years since Mr. H. E. Weatherly brought in the last rod-caught bluefin tuna. Since then this relatively warm-blooded fish has been considered extinct in the North Sea, wiped out by the uncontrolled predations of commercial fishing boats from the Continent.

The extinction theory has been challenged many times. A couple of years ago John Bennett, author of *Big Game Angling*, wrote to *Angler's Mail* from Canada. 'Science,' he said, 'leans to the view that bluefin form a single species with world-wide distribution. The total destruction of existing stocks in the North Sea would be made good by migrating fish.'

His point seems indisputable. Could it be that the combination of commercial catches plus some cyclic change— water temperature, perhaps, or the evolution of more attractive conditions elsewhere—reduced our tunny population to zero levels? Whatever the answer, tunny fishing had a short life and an expensive one.

It is only 40 years since British anglers first discussed taking these monster fish on rod and line; since L. Mitchell-Henry (holder of the British record with an 851 lb. bluefin tuna taken off Whitby) and Lt. Col. Stapleton-Colton visited Scarborough to explore the possibilities of sport in that area.

In 1929 they hooked two fish. Both tunny escaped. In 1930 Mitchell-Henry returned and on August 27 he caught the first tunny ever taken by a sport fisherman in British waters. It weighed 560 lb. His record fish took the bait just three years later.

Perhaps the finest series of catches recorded during the 25 years of productive tunny fishing in the North Sea was that of Jack Tansey of Skegness. His first fish, a 526-pounder, was boated in 1947, 18 miles east-north-east of Scarborough. Within the next two years he accounted for 14 fish. And when he died recently the cast of that first tunny, Tansey's rod, reel, line and gaff, were accepted for permanent display by Scarborough's Museum of Natural History.

Like any other branch of angling, tunny fishing in our waters is peppered with hard-luck stories, not least the experience of a man who is seldom featured in the somewhat repetitive accounts published from time to time: Mr. J. H. Lewis.

In August, 1949, Lewis landed a fish scaling 852 lb. He claimed the record and looked like getting it until *The Fishing Gazette* of September 2, 1950, pointed out that when his fish was weighed it was suspended from the scales by a rope or 'becket', the weight of which was included in the claim figure. 'In view of this,' ruled *The Gazette*, 'it cannot be accepted as beating the existing record of 851 lb. held since 1933.' The weight of a piece of rope! You cannot get closer than that.

By comparison with this class of fishing, catching porbeagles and blues of average size looks more like saltwater pimping. The views of Bill Pashby, Scarborough's most successful tunny skipper, are on record and most unlikely to please my South-Country friends. 'A tunny will test the best angler who ever wet a line,' said Bill. 'Shark? Shark can't fight: they give in too quickly. Any angler worth his name can tire one out in ten minutes.'

Be that as it may, the vast herring shoals are still there, the tunny's forage fish. And if there is truth in the rumour that bluefin tuna are back in numbers, what are the chances for future expeditions?

Eric Horsfall Turner devoted much of his younger days to the search for tunny. He recalls that each trip involved being at sea for up to a month. And when Winston Hall interviewed Bill Pashby two years ago there was talk of boats—or should it be 'ships'?—fitted with state rooms, showers and carrying a first-class chef on board. 'Today,' said Bill, 'it couldn't be done under £600 a week.' Millionaire fishing with a vengeance.

With respect, I suggest that Bill Pashby's assessment of costs and tuna searches is based on the experience of yesteryear. Tunny fishing will still be a rich man's sport, but with ship to shore radio links, helicopter services and really fast game boats, I would have thought that a well-organised expedition could cut costs and time-corners.

For a world record they have to beat more than Mitchell-Henry's 851 lb. Unless a recent claim has been submitted, the No. 1 weight is still held by Nova Scotia with a fish of 977 lb. But the 1,000-pounder is out there, perhaps cleaving the waters of the North Sea at this very moment. If anyone is thinking of following-up the whispers that have come my way they haven't much time. Scarborough's once-popular tunny season opens in August each year. It closes in October.

BASS, BRIT AND BATTLESHIPS

It was one of the hottest days of the year. John Harris's fast cruiser—an 18 ft. Crestliner with cabin forward, a spacious cockpit aft and a 75 hp outboard to push her along—sped through Portsmouth Harbour towards the Solent.

Away to our left sailing dinghies fluttered round an enormous aircraft carrier moored at one of the jetties. Far off to the right—or should it be to starboard?—a long line of silver-grey craft, cruisers and miscellaneous vessels of war, stood guard along the creek.

And then we saw the gulls; wheeling, screaming, diving into the main channel stretching ahead of us. John slowed the engine, then cut and drifted.

'Bass!' he exclaimed. 'And mackerel. Just look at them, John.'

I *was* looking, eyes popping out of my head, hand reaching for the little spinning rod set up in readiness for such situations. We were floating above an incoming stream of brit, tiny fish only two or three inches long. In their tens of thousands they were swimming in from the sea, a seemingly never-ending wall of them, three yards wide and many feet deep in the green, sunlit waters below us.

The gulls, bass and mackerel were having a ball, slashing into the brit as though they would never eat again once this harvest was over. Fragments of dead fish floated past and our presence seemed of no consequence to the hunters or their prey. It was an incredible sight. But the brit pressed on regardless of the slaughter, a well-regulated pathway of little fish intent on reaching sheltered water upstream.

We spun through and beyond them again and again, using black spoons, silver spoons, spoons large and small. I had one definite knock, that's all. With such a surfeit of natural food the big fish had neither time nor inclination to experiment with foreign bodies.

John pressed the starter button and we roared forward once more, towards the forts guarding the Solent, heading for a mark known to Portsmouth anglers as 'The Blocks'. There we took bass to 3 lb. and lone mackerel—1½ pounders, fat as butter—that fought deep and hard, surfacing with their gorgeous colours, greens and blues and oystershell pinks, gleaming in the sunlight.

And as we fished, John told me of the problems he'd faced after winning the first leg of his club's bass competition two years before. It was a decisive win—about 20 lb. of fish against an average 4-5 lb. from other competitors. But the other lads felt that he had too much of an advantage. In his boat, John could get to 'The Blocks' easily. He could run to Langstone Harbour to collect live sand eels. Acknowledging the protests, the Committee banned offshore fishing and insisted that the remaining legs of the contest be fished inside the harbour.

John fished inside, and won.

Last season there were no restrictions, but Johnny Harris was concerned that he should be thought to have any advantage. If live sand eels were going to cause trouble he would use frozen baits whenever he fished offshore. After all, everyone could buy those easily enough. It was a fair decision, especially as his clubmates had little faith in frozen eels—I can't think why. We fished them on the flood tide using outfits any freshwater angler would be happy to handle, and we had fish in plenty.

The rig used was a simple sliding leger; a bored bullet stopped 5 ft. from the 2/0 hook by a swivel joining a trace of lower breaking strain than the reel line.

There were two problems: finding the depth at which the fish were moving, and judging the weight needed to hold our baits in position. Both factors changed as the day progressed. But those baits, fished sink-and-draw or held in the tidal stream on a static line, proved most effective.

'Preserved eels I don't like,' said John, 'but these frozen baits are winners. They're even better after dark. A dead sand eel appears to give off more phosphorescence than a live one. Don't ask me why!' (This may be the case. It makes one wonder if fluorescent plugs and such aids as Efgeeco's fluorescent plastic strips have yet to be fully appreciated.)

Back in the harbour for the last hour before returning to London, I set up float tackle and trotted down on the tide to add one more species to the weekend's catch. Wrasse: green wrasse, like fish from tropical waters. Wiped out in that dreadful winter of 1963, it's nice to see them coming back again.

PICK UP: SALT DOWN

Prevailing winds along the South Coast have had an easterly bite since early January. At the end of March they changed dramatically as a sou'westerly, approaching gale force at times, took nearly three days to blow itself out. Sea mists followed; dank grey shrouds enveloping cliff top and beach, surf and breakwater.

Armed with a canvas bucket, I set off in search of slipper limpets. It's a strange thing that although choirs of anglers sing the praises of mussel, lug and ragworm, few acknowledge the value of this shellfish from overseas. Yet the slipper limpet is a splendid bait for bass and flatfish; a bait that needs no digging and is to be had, free of charge, along much of the South Coast and in many North Sea areas.

There are two versions of how it came to us from America. The most likely is that the limpets were brought over with live oysters and introduced to the Thames Estuary before the 1914-18 war. Others tell of an American cargo boat tipping unwanted ballast—tons of shingle from a distant beach—into Southampton Water. Mixed with that shingle were the ancestors of the creatures I collected that morning.

I'm told that slipper limpets normally live below the low-water mark. But when a stormy sea scours the bottom and hurls much of it high on to the beach, thousands of these limpets are left stranded. Most single shells are empty. Why this should be I know not, unless it is that seabirds and other predators make quick work of a meal so obviously exposed. In the mist that morning I stood for some minutes watching a solitary crow walking stiff-legged along the flotsam line, turning likely-looking shells with its beak and stabbing here and there at something too distant for me to see, but almost certainly an unfortunate slipper limpet. He and I were in the same business.

For the angler, clusters of shells are a guarantee of hookbait. You will find two, three or even half-a-dozen locked one on top of the other. The bottom shell is invariably empty or replaced by a pebble forming a foundation stone for the entire colony.

Once you have the knack, and have learned not to slice your thumb in half, average-sized slipper limpets are not too difficult to prise apart. A strong knife is essential. Nick the point of the blade under the bend at the 'tail end' of the topmost shell and give a slow, firm twist. Specimen limpets need different treatment. If the knife is resisted, use the handle as a hammer and tap round the shell where it joins the one below. This usually loosens them.

Lifting a limpet from its shell without damage is a somewhat dainty operation. The yellow-hued foot, the tough part with which the shellfish clings to its neighbour, is now fully exposed and lies on a saucer-shaped platform covering two-thirds of the shell opening. Inside, a soft tongue shelters at the back of the shell.

Run the tip of your knife round the edge of the foot, being sure to place it between the outer skin, known as the mantle, and the smooth shell. Then scrape the foot away from its platform and ease out the entire limpet. Two or three of them make a very good bait indeed.

As an emergency standby I've salted some down in a polythene jar—although any jar will do—layers of common salt alternating with layers of limpets. These reserve baits harden considerably in salt, and this is their main disadvantage, but they seem to soften after a period in the water and are best used as one of a mixed bait with fresh and preserved limpets placed alternately on the hook.

STARFISH MAKE A NICE CHANGE!

It may seem a far cry from the scientist studying marine ecology to the angler setting out for a few hours' cod fishing. But in one sense the gap is not really so great. Knowing how fish behave is important whether you aim to increase the world's food supply or boost the family budget with a nice 12-pounder.

In 1969 a Canadian researcher published some fascinating details concerning the feeding habits of the cod family. Much of his findings dispel the picture of the cod as an animated trawl, ploughing through the water with its mouth wide open, engulfing everything in its path. When it's down on the sea bed the cod is anything but a crude feeder.

Did you know, for example, that this fish can taste food with its fins? Like the barbule under its chin, a cod's pelvic fins are decked with taste buds. When there is nothing moving off the bottom the fish has no option but to search for its food—'tasting' the sea bed. This it does by nosing downwards with the chin barbule and its two pelvic fins feeling their way along the sand, gravel or rock.

It may be that these fins are the least sensitive of the cod's taste organs, for when they react to food the fish stops, goes into reverse and re-locates the tit-bit with its barbule. It then mouths the food, testing it yet again before swallowing.

Most important from an angler's point of view, the cod's sense of smell is extremely sensitive and plays a major part in its search for crabs, seaworms and various shellfish. It has been established that in their natural state these creatures give off body odours which hungry cod follow like Bisto Kids on their way home. Not that marine creatures lie around waiting to be picked off by passing predators! They bury themselves as deeply as possible. But that body odour is their undoing, and a few inches of gravel present no problems to a codfish.

Having found the approximate source of food, the cod sticks its tail 'in the air' and removes stones and sand, mouthfuls at a time, until the food is exposed. Faced with quite large stones a cod will shovel them aside with its head, relying on its sense of smell to keep unnecessary work to a minimum. Vivien Brawn, the scientist who published this data, says: 'Food animals which swim up off the bottom are easily seen by cod during the day, and adult cod can capture such food even when it is as small as two millimetres across. *Once food has settled on the bottom only much larger pieces are detected by sight.*' (The italics are mine, for obvious reasons—J.P.)

It must follow that the man who takes time off to dope his baits with herring oil—and herring is a favourite food of cod the world over—is loading the scales to advantage. His fish may not see the bait, but there is every chance that they will smell it and move to investigate. In a less precise sense the same applies to a boat's rubby-dubby bag.

As one might expect, food selection varies with the age and size of the fish concerned. Research into the stomach contents of 280 cod of all sizes revealed that while young fish held only 10 per cent fish food, 81 per cent crustacea and 9 per cent other matter, the diet of fully-grown cod consisted of 69 per cent fish, 16 per cent crustacea and 15 per cent other matter.

One odd fact emerged. While cod of all ages choose a mixed diet fairly rich in calories—in human terms it is said to be on a par with beef stew, mashed potato or tapioca pudding—large specimens make a point of occasionally feasting on foods of low energy value. Vivien Brawn quotes the brittle starfish as an example and suggests that it may contain some mineral element not provided by the normal diet.

Herring, squid, shellfish or stars? Never be surprised if the next record cod falls for liver sausage or even a banana skin.

But if you are fishing the bottom, remember one thing: bait scents make sense. That's a scientific fact!

PREDATORY MULLET

Mullet on light tackle are great little fighters, and at Christchurch they mingle throughout the summer and autumn with a fine run of sea trout. It's a journey I often make.

There can be no hard and fast rules about mullet. They differ greatly, in so many ways, from one locality to another. For example, one writer insists that mullet are not worth eating. The only commercial market, he says, is provided by zoos with seals to feed. Perhaps the fish in his area are preoccupied with food that taints their flesh: mine are delicious, and the French cannot get enough of them.

Another doubtful point is the assertion that all mullet are 'soft-lipped'. The Christchurch fish seem anything but. Nor is there truth in the advice, repeated *ad nauseum* for half a century or more, that the only way to catch mullet is to fish fragments of soft bait on tiny hooks and ultra-fine tackle. And are all mullet populations easily scared? They may be at some venues, but those I contact in Christchurch and Poole Harbours are not readily put down.

Writing in *Angler's Mail*, Arnold Wiles told how he first took fish on the traditional mullet spoons used along this part of the coast. The key to success, he said, is that spinners only produce results when baited with pieces of ragworm, harbour rag. True, that is the advice freely and genuinely given by local anglers, but other baits work just as well: there's nothing special about rag. Indeed, I have known these fish to hit and hold an unbaited size 6 treble trailed behind a spinning vane 2½ in. long.

All this has nothing to do with the way mullet become accustomed to unnatural foods, such as bread waste from waterside cafes or milk slops from a dairy bordering the estuary. To my mind, it is proof positive that in the natural state they do not feed *only* on algae, as has been suggested. They do *not* eat nothing but mud-dwelling creatures—tiny shellfish, ragworm and bloodworms, as others believe. Their diet is a mixed one and I suspect that they are themselves a mixture of scavenger and predator—more predatory than we have been led to expect.

From the angler's point of view one definite fact emerges: baited spoons catch far more mullet than those without baits. When I first heard of the need to use ragworm I pondered the advice given and decided that it had to be wrong. After all why should rag trailed behind a metal lure have more attraction than any other hookbait?

I used ragworm for the first few trips, with marked success, as local club members had predicted. And having got the feel of things I stopped digging rag, bought a few maggots and impaled one on each barb of the treble hook. I caught just as many mullet as before.

It did not seem to matter whether one spun a size 'O' Droppen or a No. 3 Mepps. Both caught fish if the maggots were firmly in place.

It is my belief that the flash of the spoon attracts these fish initially. If they were merely curious they would follow the spoon in, but no more. As it is, they move to investigate, attack and throw the hook with remarkable speed *if there is nothing worth holding on to*. I've known mullet hit unbaited spoons with tremendous force, bending the rod hard over and convincing the angler that his fish is 'on'. Seconds later the line goes slack.

I have baited successfully with snippets of rag, lobworm and brandling, as well as maggot. It may be that minute pieces of lug or fish-strip on the treble will also persuade a hungry mullet not to let go.

Some anglers state categorically that mullet in their waters will not touch a spinner. As like as not, baited spoons have never been tried. I simply cannot accept that there is anything so completely exceptional about the fish in Christchurch Har-

bour. If they take spinners so will other mullet. The exceptions
may be those preoccupied with food peculiar to a given locality,
for it does seem that with this species the theory of preoccupa-
tion has a special significance.

Christchurch mullet are caught on wet flies, but so are those
elsewhere; one more proof of their predatory nature. And after
watching them feed on many calm and sunny evenings, I have
no doubt they will take a dry fly at times. That's on my list
for summer fishing in 1970!

It would be interesting to hear from readers who have tried
baited spoons in other waters: successful or not. The only
reference I have is a brief note in John Garrad's book, *Sea
Angling with the Baited Spoon*. He records that a Mr. Ether-
ington, trolling a 3 in. baited spoon for flounder in Portsmouth
Harbour, hooked and boated a grey mullet of 1¾ lb.

The scientists have recently revised the Latin names of 29
species of saltwater fish common to our waters, thin- and thick-
lipped mullet among them. The thin-lipped species, originally
Mugil tamada or *Mugil capito*, has become *Chelon ramada*. Its
thick-lipped cousin, once *Mugil labrosus* or *Mugil chelo*, is now
Crenimugil labrosus. You will find the full list in Clive Gam-
mon's book, *Sea Fishing*, published by Pelham Books, price
42s. It is, in fact, the only book with such an up-to-date list—
one of many reasons why I consider it the finest reference work
available to sea anglers.

Whatever scientists may do with Latin names, the mullet
is one fish about which anglers can still contribute much-needed
knowledge. The majority of the data so far recorded, by scientists and anglers alike, is decidedly suspect in some instances
and in others positively inaccurate!

HERMIT IN THE SAND

The Lugworm, *Arenicola marina*, is one of the largest and most abundant worms of the seashore, for which anglers have every reason to be grateful. These distant relatives of the common earthworm spend their entire lives in solitary confinement, happy to be restricted to a 'U'-shaped tunnel reaching only twelve inches, seldom more, below the surface. Some inhabit a 'straight down' shaft, no less solitary. Which poses an interesting question: how do they manage to produce young?

Six species of lug provide the millions that inhabit the world's coastlines. Suitable beaches in both hemispheres are peppered with their traces—casts, each separated by a few inches from a depression in the sand as though the surface was about to subside, which in all truth, it is!

Contrary to popular belief, the lugworm does not eat the sand as it shapes its burrow. It bulldozes its way down, pushing loose, damp sand behind it and to either side until the 'tail shaft' is complete. At 10-14 in. below the surface the worm turns to construct the level section—the most important part of its burrow and the nearest thing to home it will ever know. In this the walls are strengthened with a light coating of sand and mucus—a cement, if you like—to prevent the tunnel from collapsing. This achieved, the worm then works upwards to form the 'head shaft'. The entire operation requires from 24 to 48 hours before the owner is safely in residence and ready for a square meal.

A lugworm eats sand as everyone knows, but its main interest is in the plankton and traces of organic matter trapped *on the surface* when the tide goes out. Its larder is constantly replenished by sand falling into the head shaft. This it digests, cleans and passes into the tail section of its body. The segmented tail is then pushed to the surface where it deposits unwanted grains in the form of cylinders or ropes of sand—the tell-tale casts we know so well.

The odd shape of the lugworm, with its thick body and relatively long, thin tail, provides a further example of the super-efficiency of evolutionary development. All the vital organs are housed in the main part of the body. The tail is nothing more than a living tube, muscular, nerve sensitive and formed of segments that can be replaced when necessary. And it often is necessary, for this is the part exposed to attack by crabs, birds and other enemies as it ejects digested sand at the surface.

To the lugworm food is important, but oxygen is even more vital. When incoming seawater covers its burrow there is no problem. By expanding its body it can block the lower tunnel completely. As fresh water runs over and into the burrow the worm draws a supply from the tail shaft and then, by swelling and contracting its body segments, it literally *pumps* a constant flow of oxygenated water until the tide turns. This process keeps the occupant in A.1 condition. It also cleanses and strengthens the tunnel.

With the outgoing tide life becomes more difficult. The lugworm can exist without oxygen for a few hours only. At low tide it often draws its supply from moist air trapped in the shafts, wriggling towards the surface to absorb as much oxygen as possible before returning to the dead water in the main tunnel. It is claimed that as the tide turns the lug thrusts its tail above the sand and takes down a bubble of air to augment its oxygen supply. This may be true. Freshwater carp are said to hold air bubbles against their gills whenever the oxygen content of the water falls to a dangerously low level. The lugworm's body contains an exceptional amount of blood and this, too, plays a part in providing life-preserving supplies of oxygen.

Considerable research has been carried out on this strange creature, with special reference to its value as cleaner and irrigator-in-chief of our shorelands. Professor G. P. Wells, a noted expert, estimates that 'in one square yard of a densely-populated beach, over a gallon of water is driven to a depth of a foot or more and rises to the surface again in every hour'.

Each lugworm is either male or female—unlike the lob, which is an hermaphrodite and able to act as either sex. Which brings us back to my opening question: how do these solitary individuals reproduce the species?

A lugworm prizes personal safety above all else. Nothing will tempt it from its tunnel unless there is absolutely no alternative. Even the future of the world's lugworm supplies is subject to this over-riding consideration. *Arenicola* spawns once a year, during the autumn months in the British Isles, when male and female edge backwards into their respective tail shafts and deposit not casts of unwanted sand but sperm or eggs at the surface. The incoming tide does the rest—carrying, mixing, fertilising and ensuring the next generation. Hit-and-miss it may be, but it works!

DENTS IN THE SEA BED

Jazzeen is not a big boat. Her owner, John Harris of Fareham, calls her 'a pocket cruiser'. At 18 ft. from nose to stern, powered by a single 75 hp outboard, that's a fair description. She is not an all-weather boat for the open sea, but John had for some time nurtured a pet theory that could only be proved or disproved by ranging far from land.

In an area as heavily fished as the Solent and neighbouring waters, big bags are by no means commonplace. John was convinced that one solution lay in finding depressions in the sea bed that no anglers have yet discovered and that commercial fishermen would avoid for fear of damaging their nets.

'The depressions are there,' he once told me, 'and they must hold a real payload—big fish of all kinds.'

To my certain knowledge, Johnny Harris is not lacking in courage. But he is not suicidal. In such a boat the trip could only be made in near-perfect conditions, settled weather guaranteeing time for the outward run, exploration and the return voyage from points 14 miles or more from land. He fitted an echo-sounder to Jazzeen and waited, patiently.

He waited for some months until the barometer, the Met Office forecasters and his own knowledge of weather lore reached the same conclusion. Set Fair: the sea as calm as a park lake. It was July, 1968.

Visibility was superb, the sky cloudless and the water that shade of blue seen on picture postcards from Italy and other parts of the Mediterranean. Jazzeen moved gracefully from her moorings in Portchester Creek, through the east Solent on to open water approaching the Nab Tower. Whether you fish for gudgeon or trout, bass or conger, there come those rare days when you know darned well that exceptional sport lies ahead. For John, that July morning was such an occasion.

With his little boat eating up distance at her top speed of 30 knots, he stood at the controls revelling in the sunshine; the clear air and the brilliance around him was something to marvel at. 'The wake behind me looked like a colour advert for someone's detergent; snow-white on a blue background.'

The journey to the Nab Tower—a sea fort guarding the approaches to Portsmouth—took 45 minutes. Noting such things was important, for if the weather should change it would be as well to know the time needed for the return journey. It doesn't do to take chances when roving far out in a small boat. He cut the engine, set up compass and chart, and switched on the echo-sounder; then headed out at a steady speed, bearing on a channel of deep water that lay some miles distant between two banks.

The operation was well under way when the echo-sounder gave notice that the bottom was shelving, dropping sharply from 40 ft. to 60 ft., levelling out at this depth and then, after 50 yds. or so, rising again to the overall level of the surrounding area. Here was a narrow gulley, probably unknown to any other boat; a tiny strip of the sea bed that may never have been fished before.

Throttle down: turn about. Slowly, the engine just ticking over, John traversed this dent in the bottom, his eyes fixed on the graph paper of his echo-sounder.

'I was praying that it would be too rough for trawling. It was!' A firm re-echo line showed the sea bed to be hard. An erratic graph indicated a rough, uneven bottom that no netsman in his right mind would ever think of trawling.

Angling fever set in. It seemed an eternity, an inexcusable delay, just waiting for the anchor rope to run out. And that delay brought its own doubts and fears. Supposing, after all these months and having found a seemingly perfect spot, he failed to catch mackerel to bait the hook? Imagine sitting all day above virgin fishing ground angling for hookbait! The haste with which he paid out the mackerel line brought him back to reality with a yelp. A trickle of blood ran from his left hand, a sure reminder that it does not do to hurry these things or let the imagination run riot.

The bait line reacted to one thumping knock after another and within minutes four shining mackerel—fish of such gorgeous colours that few housewives would recognise them—lay in the well of the boat. John filleted a whole side of one fish, slid it on to an 8/0 hook, back-barbed and crimped to a 5 ft. steel trace, and lowered it gently into the clear water. The bait flapped enticingly in the steadily-flowing tide. Skate, tope, conger? Bait and tackle were enough for any one of them; he hadn't come this far to catch pout whiting.

Still the mackerel came up, enough for the day's bait and a few for supper, until the jigger was put away. There was no point in risking a tangle with a hard-fighting tope. His tackle in position, John lit a cigarette, and as he did so the reel started to tick ... and tick ... and tick as a fish moved off with the bait. A strike, a brief fight against his game rod and the first thornback came to the gaff. Five minutes later, another. Then a third, a 15-pounder.

Three skates in less than an hour seemed good going. Thinking to celebrate with a cup of coffee, he put the kettle on. Fatal. The reel gave a screech and John grabbed for his rod, to fight a tope 'as big as any I've ever played'. No doubt it was, but Johnny Harris was destined never to boat that fish. It broke him, the last few feet of line frayed by its sandpaper hide.

Disappointment was short-lived as another good skate and some dogfish came aboard. Forget the kettle; who wants coffee anyway? There's only one thing to do in these circumstances— keep fishing. And this he did for eight memorable hours until the setting sun and a well full of fish warned him that home and the little boat's moorings lay far away.

A check at the Clubhouse scales showed his total catch as 10 skate and 35 assorted dogfish, total weight 170 lb. It had been a wonderful day's sport, I think deservedly so, for if ever a trip was planned to the last hopeful detail, this was it.

A chart, an echo-sounder, settled weather conditions and a dent in the sea bed. You know, there might be a few undis- covered dents in your area!

A LINK WITH BOYHOOD

Angling, they say, is a sport that keeps you young. I agree. And if it doesn't strike you that way you're concentrating on the wrong kind of fishing. Get a sea rod, a roach pole or a fly rod. Turn freelance, take up match fishing or join a big-fish group. There's a niche for you somewhere.

To what extent the sport can check the ageing process is not for me to say. I suppose it has something to do with one's boyhood days: with the ability to re-live the problems that still face young anglers: to thrill to events that make no im- pression on the not-so-young at heart.

Take a recent news item. Take a look at tousle-haired young Nicky West of Ryde, in the Isle of Wight. He learned the meaning of pride, heartbreak and glorious, unexpected success

—albeit a trifle fortunate—within the space of a few hours.

Nicky is a sea angler. His 14th birthday present was a marvellous new rod and reel. Imagine the joy such a gift must bring. Imagine the secret plans, the unspoken hopes as that outfit was set up and tried out at home. With such tackle no record was safe!

So, with confidence amounting to near-certainty, our angler set off to fish the seawall at Appley. The new rod had still that unaccustomed feel. Not that any stranger would be aware of that! At 14 one acts as a thoroughly experienced fisherman, while making sure that neither dents nor scratches mar the sparkling new fittings and varnish.

Nicky cast out, his beloved rod behaving perfectly. Of course they'd take record fish together! He may have been dreaming of just such a feat when rod and reel were snatched from his hands—yes, snatched!—and disappeared into the sea. Can YOU react to the shock of that moment: your most prized possession gone, taken by a fish and a monster at that after all you had told yourself about specimens and techniques and what a fine angler you'd be?

But Nicky West wasn't beaten yet. There was a fair chance that when the tide went out his rod would be found. For all that, one dreadful notion was not to be denied. That fish must have been a whopper: by now, it and the rod could be half-way to the French coast. There was nothing for it but to wait, and under these circumstances waiting involves an agonising appraisal of one's own shortcomings. Did our fisherman kick his toecaps against the seawall? Perhaps. Did he accuse N. West of being a blithering idiot, a downright rotten angler? I guess so.

That day, Nicky West learned how fickle the Lords of the Rod can be. When at last the tide receded there lay his precious tackle, none the worse for its spell below-water. And struggling at the end of the line was the biggest bass this young man had ever encountered. Relief—and what relief!—turned to heart-pounding excitement, for playing that fish through the surf was an experience never to be forgotten.

Bass of 8½ lb. are not taken every day, nor does the sport

always provide a happy ending and one's picture in the country's finest angling paper. But that's how this story ended in December, 1966. Since then I've met a number of youngsters—one in his 70s, several topping the half-century and a few juniors of 30-plus—who have lived this boy's story as if, in their imagination, each of them had been the leading character. For such people angling is not a matter of trophies, cash and kudos. To them and Nicky West—to all who find in their sport a link with the things that really matter—I extend our time-honoured greeting for the years ahead ... Tight Lines!